CW00417365

A GH
ON TIPTOE

A Comedy

ROBERT MORLEY
and
ROSEMARY ANNE SISSON

SAMUEL  FRENCH

LONDON
NEW YORK   TORONTO   SYDNEY   HOLLYWOOD

Please note our NEW ADDRESS:

Samuel French Ltd
52 Fitzroy Street London W1P 6JR
Tel: 01 - 387 9373

A GHOST ON TIPTOE

First presented by Ray Cooney Productions at the Savoy Theatre, London, on the 25th April 1974, with the following cast of characters:

Barnstable	Robert Morley
Henry Poole	William Franklyn
Mrs Barnstable	Joyce Carey
Nora Barnstable	Ambrosine Phillpotts
Selena	Delia Lindsay
Roger	Christopher Matthews
Poppy	Karin Fernald
Stubbs	Richard Ommanney

Directed by Jan Butlin

The action takes place in the sitting-room of Cuthbert Barnstable's house in West London

ACT I
    Scene 1   Autumn
    Scene 2   A month later

ACT II
    Scene 1   Spring
    Scene 2   A month later

Time – the present

ACT I

SCENE 1

The sitting-room of Barnstable's house in Fulham. Autumn

The room is agreeably and comfortably furnished. French windows lead to the garden, and double doors to the dining-room, from which another door, unseen, leads to the hall. There is also another, single, door that leads to the hall and the rest of the house direct

Henry is standing facing the garden, looking at some X-rays. Barnstable stands watching him. There is a bottle of brandy and two brandy balloons on the coffee-table. There is a long pause

Barnstaple Say something.

Henry I don't know how you got hold of these.

Barnstable I bought them.

Henry You can't buy X-rays.

Barnstable Why not? I didn't do this on the National Health, you know. I went to the top. Chap called Rolls; heard of him?

Henry No.

Barnstable He had gilt horses harnessed to a chariot on his mantelpiece. I don't pretend I found him particularly reassuring.

Henry It seems extraordinary, him telling you right out like that. I suppose you didn't misunderstand him?

Barnstable No, he was quite definite, once he'd started. I had a bit of a job to make him tell me what was wrong. He said he wanted to have another look at the X-rays and then he'd write to my chap. I told him he hadn't done his homework. He didn't like that much. One thing led to another. Finally, I told him that if he didn't know what was wrong it would be more honest of him to say so right away. Then, of course, he said he knew perfectly well, and we had another row about him not wanting to say. I made it pretty obvious that I wasn't going to leave until I found out the truth, and he obviously had patients piling up in his waiting-room, and at last he cracked.

Henry Cracked?

Barnstable Lost his temper and blurted out the whole thing. I was saying something about how doctors loved to keep people in suspense, and that it gave them a power complex, and that I, personally, hadn't the time for all that nonsense, and he suddenly agreed with me.

Henry How do you mean, agreed?

Barnstable "You're damned right", he said, "you haven't the time.

You've got a year", he said. "Eighteen months at the most." (*He puts X-rays in a book*)

Henry What are you doing? Pressing them?

Barnstable I'm putting them away. I don't want everybody looking at them. Nobody ever opens the *Encyclopaedia Britannica* in this house. It's my filing system. All one has to do is to remember the page. "E" for Enema.

Henry But why, exactly? Did Rolls say why?

Barnstable Yes, it's Blum's Disease. Imagine a trampoline, Henry.

Henry Why should I?

Barnstable That's how Rolls explained it. The trampoline is faulty. Each time I bounce on it I bounce a little higher, until one day . . .

Henry You go out through the roof?

Barnstable No, I go down through the trampoline.

Henry Can't they mend the trampoline?

Barnstable Apparently not, in my case. He said if I lost a bit of weight and took care, it might delay matters for a few weeks. I shan't bother.

Henry Of course you will!

Barnstable No, I shan't. I haven't got a lot to live for. I suppose I haven't had a bad life, but I'm not particularly interested in carrying on with it. There is one thing I regret.

Henry (*rather moved*) What's that, Barney?

Barnstable I wish I'd gone into property. I'd've made a fortune round here. Nora will be able to sell this house for ten times what I gave for it. She'll be glad. She never liked it. Do you think I ought to tell her?

Henry You mean what the house is worth?

Barnstable No, no, no. About Blum's Disease. I thought I'd leave her a note.

Henry Afterwards? She'll know by then. They all will.

Barnstable Yes, but if I tell them now they might tell Mother.

Henry You'll never be able to keep it from *her*. You've never kept anything from her in your life.

Barnstable Of course I have.

Henry Such as?

Barnstable (*pondering*) She doesn't know my profits.

Henry Nor do you, until the accountants do the books.

Barnstable I've a rough idea.

Henry So has your mother. Not so rough, either.

Mother enters from the double doors, and goes to get a newspaper from the coffee table

Ask her.

Mother Have you finished with the brandy, dear?

Barnstable Leave it, Mother.

Mother It's not very good for you and it's certainly not very good for Henry. He has to work this afternoon.

Barnstable *I'm* not going to work. Leave it, dear.

Mother I'll just put it away, then if you must have another one you'll know where it is.

She puts the brandy away in the cupboard

Barnstable I knew where it was when it was on the table.
Henry Ask her.
Mother Ask me what?
Barnstable Mother, what did the business make last year?
Mother What did the business make? Think, dear, think!
Barnstable I don't have to think. I *know*. It's my business.
Mother Then why do you ask me?
Barnstable To settle an argument with Henry.
Mother You want me to tell Henry?
Barnstable Yes.
Mother Well, he made twenty-seven thousand pounds.
Henry Did he?

Mother goes to the double doors

Mother He declared fifteen.

Mother exits

Barnstable Quite inaccurate.
Henry How much did you make?
Barnstable I wouldn't dream of telling you. It's confidential. There won't be any profits when I go, that's for sure. At least Roger will realize what a fool he's been. Even if he didn't want to work in the business, he could have been a director—carried on with someone else running it.
Henry He can still do that.
Barnstable No, he can't. I've left instructions for it to be sold.
Henry I thought you said it wasn't worth anything.
Barnstable Are you trying to annoy me?
Henry Sorry.
Barnstable You'd have thought that having a son of his own would have given Roger some sense of responsiblity, but since Adam was born he's been worse. He was supposed to pick up Adam from a party the other day. Had his head in the clouds as usual, and picked up the wrong child. Of course that wife of his is perfectly useless. When Roger told me he was going to marry an art student, I never dreamt she planned to make a career of it.
Henry They do nowadays.
Barnstable Five bloody years she's been at College. I asked her the other day how much longer. "I'm in no hurry", she said. Talk about business-men on the fiddle, these students can teach us a thing or two, I'll tell you that.
Henry I thought you liked her.
Barnstable I'm sorry for her. I'm sorry for anyone married to my son.
Henry Anyway, Nora and your mother enjoy having Adam here.

Barnstable I daresay they do. That's not the point. Do you think that child is backward?

Henry No of course not.

Barnstable He is. Can't mention it to anyone in this home, of course. They'd fly off the handle. But I'm sure I was talking quite clearly at fifteen months.

Henry I expect you were.

Barnstable What's that supposed to mean? Am I boring you?

Henry Not at all. But I think you're being a bit tough on Roger.

Barnstable How would you like your son to be a Municipal Baths attendant?

Henry I wouldn't mind if it suited him. He plans to be a writer.

Barnstable Eighteen pounds a week.

Henry That's what he gets now.

Barnstable It's what he'll always get, until he's too old for a bucket and broom and they pension him off. That child went to Westminster.

Henry What about it?

Barnstable Not quite the return one expects for an investment like that.

Henry You don't invest in your children.

Barnstable So I found. Just as well. It makes it easier to say good-bye to the lot of them. I've made you my executor, by the way.

Henry Oh, that's very nice of you.

Barnstable Not at all. You and the bank. I wish to be buried at sea.

Henry Let's discuss it when the time comes, shall we?

Barnstable I don't think you're listening.

Henry I am.

Barnstable When the time comes, I shall be dead. That's why we will be having a funeral. I want my ashes scattered off Dover.

Henry Why?

Barnstable That's where I was born.

Henry Off Dover? Was your mother a cross-channel swimmer?

Barnstable Not off, in. Perhaps I'd better leave the arrangements to the bank.

Henry No, it's just that it struck me as being rather—whimsical.

Barnstable I don't think I've ever been called whimsical before.

Henry I suppose that's what surprised me.

Barnstable You can hire a small launch and charge it to the estate.

Henry Not too small. It has to be three miles out.

Barnstable Henry, we're talking about last rites, not fishing rights.

Henry Anyway, I'll find out.

Henry takes a notebook out of his pocket and writes in it. Barnstable watches him doubtfully

Barnstable I don't want a lot of flowers. You can buy a small wreath and drop it on the waves.

Henry Yes. If it turns out to be very rough, would you have any objection if I just took a little walk along the beach? With the wreath, of course.

Barnstable Yes, I would. I'd have the greatest possible objection. I don't want to end up on the shingle among the bottles and french letters.
Henry But it'll be winter.
Barnstable We don't know for certain.
Henry I suppose I can always take Kwells. Do you want a party afterwards?
Barnstable A celebration?
Henry No—a few drinks for your friends. Cheers people up.
Barnstable They won't want cheering up. I can count on one hand the people who will come to my funeral.
Henry Nonsense.
Barnstable I don't mind, particularly. In this world, either one is popular or one isn't. I just don't happen to be popular.
Henry You are popular. It's just that you don't encourage—intimacy.
Barnstable I don't encourage indecent exposure either.
Henry There you are—you never will discuss things seriously.
Barnstable That's very good, coming from you. I tell you I'm dying and you start planning a party.
Henry Not at all. It was you who started planning. I was just trying to fit in with your mood.
Barnstable I should have thought you'd be upset.
Henry Of course I'm upset. If . . .
Barnstable If what?
Henry If he's right. Just at this moment I find it difficult to put my thoughts into words. I've known you thirty years. I can't take it in. Put yourself in my place. Suppose the situation was reversed and I told you I had twelve months . . .
Barnstable Eighteen months. Don't let's rush the fences.
Henry That's what I mean. What does one say? I'm only just beginning to realize it. Do you mind if I have another brandy?
Barnstable Help yourself. No good saving the brandy now.
Henry If it's any comfort to you, I think you're handling this thing damn' well. Just as I would have expected. Brave as a bloody lion. To hell with the doctors, and may you live to be a hundred! I'm going to check up on this Rolls fellow. What did he say was wrong, exactly?
Barnstable It's called Blum's Disease. It's fairly rare, I believe. Why are you writing it down?
Henry So that I can make a few inquiries. Blum. Who was he, do you suppose?
Barnstable He wasn't the first patient, that's for sure. Doctors call the diseases after themselves, like mountain climbers.
Henry I suppose most people wouldn't much relish giving their names to a disease.
Barnstable I wouldn't mind if it was a good one. What do you think happens to you when you're dead?
Henry I've no idea.
Barnstable Do you suppose we go on?
Henry Well, if we do, you should be thinking about it.

Barnstable Thinking about what?

Henry What you're going to do when you do.

Barnstable Do what?

Henry Go on.

Barnstable What on earth are you talking about? If you go on, you go on.

Henry But go on doing what? Just the same as you're doing now?

Barnstable Well, I hope not. I'm expecting something a great deal better. Tell me, do you still have fun in bed?

Henry Increasingly rarely.

Barnstable But you keep your hand in? You hoist the flag occasionally?

Henry As you so delicately put it. On occasions.

Barnstable Of course, you've always gone in for it. It's practice, I suppose.

Henry Partly.

Barnstable I'd have liked to be a great lover.

Henry Wouldn't we all?

Barnstable One of my troubles has been having to get up at five o'clock the next morning. One's always conscious of it.

Henry So I should imagine.

Barnstable Of course, I married too young. I ought to have slept around more. Do you believe a man can have any woman if he puts his mind to it?

Henry I certainly think the reverse is true.

Barnstable Do women still make passes at you?

Henry All the time.

Barnstable They never have at me. Once. But everyone said she was a nymphomaniac.

Henry That put you off?

Barnstable Well, yes, I suppose it did.

Henry You made a grave mistake.

Barnstable What puzzles me is that the men who are supposed to be successful in bed are so unexpected. I can understand you in a way. You've got nice manners, and you take trouble, and you've got that lovely blazer.

Henry Thank you.

Barnstable Not at all! But most of them—we have a little chap who comes into the office—he's got red hair and the most enormous nose you ever saw. They say he never stops.

Henry Blowing it?

Barnstable Is that what they call it now?

Henry I don't know. I'll ask around.

Barnstable Sex is a sort of secret society, isn't it? A sort of Mafia. If you're not a member, you can't play. I wouldn't mind having a final blow, though. You wouldn't put me up, I suppose?

Henry I don't think I'm a member myself.

Barnstable Of course you are. You're a founder member. Would you do it?

Henry You have to ask yourself, what are they going to get out of it?

Barnstable Me for a start.

Henry Which you? You can't offer them marriage. I take it you don't want to offer them money.

Barnstable I wouldn't mind offering them money, within reason.

Henry I don't know what Nora would think.

Barnstable No, well, I don't think we'll ask Nora. Now Henry, this is a hypothetical question. Supposing I said, "Henry, I'd like to have a tumble before I push off", which of all the women you've known would be the most likely to fall for me?

Henry Of all the women I've known?

Barnstable Narrow the field a bit. Let's say, the ones who are alive now, and kicking.

Henry Thank you very much. Hypothetically?

Barnstable Hypothetically.

Henry Mm. I'll see what I can do. (*He writes in his notebook*)

Barnstable "Try Martha Hackney?"

Henry Don't expect miracles.

Barnstable Martha Hackney doesn't sound like a miracle. She sounds like a disaster area.

Henry She's a very good sport.

Barnstable How old?

Henry You can't afford to be too fussy at your age. How old are you?

Barnstable You won't believe this. I'm pushing sixty-one.

Henry looks at him

Henry Hm. That pushes Martha Hackney right out. (*He crosses the name out of the notebook*)

Barnstable Oh, Henry!

Henry I'll do the best I can. Ah, Nora!

Nora enters

Nora Mother's ready to take Adam for his walk.

Barnstable Good.

Nora Well, don't just say "good", dear. Go and help her with the pram.

Barnstable Why can't she leave the pram in the front drive? Why does she always shove it round the back?

Nora Adam prefers to be in the back garden, under the trees.

Barnstable Has he said so? Oh no, of course, he can't talk, can he?

Nora (*warningly*) Barney!

Barnstable It's quite all right. If the child is backward, he's backward. No point in trying to conceal it.

Nora He is not. . . ! (*Controlling herself*) Don't argue, dear. Just go and do as I ask.

Henry I'll go. I want to say good-bye to your Mother anyway.

Nora Barney will go. It's his grandson. Mother's expecting you to go to the park with them.

Barnstable I doubt if she does. Not after last Sunday.

Nora Why, what happened?

Barnstable We had a pile-up.

Henry A pile-up?

Barnstable A pram crash. It wasn't my fault the little fellows hadn't fastened their seat-belts.
Nora Do get on, Barney. Mother's waiting.
Barnstable Oh, all right.

Barnstable exits to the garden

Nora (*to Barnstable, as he goes*) Anyone would think you were an old man. (*To Henry*) His mother has twice the energy. Soon, she'll be pushing him in a bathchair and Adam will have to walk.
Henry I suppose, after getting up at five every morning during the week . . .
Nora Five?
Henry Six, then. I knew he was exaggerating.
Nora Barney hasn't been up at six for years.
Henry I thought he had to walk round the market and——
Nora No, of course not. He has a buyer who does all the work. He doesn't leave the house, now, till after nine.
Henry Oh.
Nora You know what he'll do when you've gone? He'll settle down in that chair with the Sunday papers and a glass of brandy, and in ten minutes he'll be sound asleep. He'll wake up at tea-time, overeat, and and go to sleep again. After dinner, he'll turn on the television and go to sleep. He'll wake up at ten and go to bed, and when I go up at midnight he'll be flat on his back, snoring. Then, at two o'clock in the morning, he'll wake me up and ask me to make him a cup of tea because he can't sleep and he's worried about his insomnia.
Henry Nora . . .

Barnstable enters

Barnstable She wants some bread for the ducks.
Nora There are some crusts in the kitchen.
Henry I'll get it. I must say good-bye to your Mother.
Barnstable Don't forget the little matter we were talking about.
Henry I still think you ought to tell Nora about that other little matter.
Barnstable (*outraged*) *Little matter?*
Henry I thought you ought to tell her. Thank you Nora for another delicious lunch as usual.
Nora I'll come and see you off, Henry.

Nora exits

Barnstable gets the Sunday papers from the table by the window, throws them on the floor round the armchair, sits, and reads one

As Barnstable reads the final newspaper Nora returns, and tidies the papers during the following scene

What little matter was that?

Barnstable What time are the children coming?

Nora I expect they'll pick up Adam about tea-time.

Barnstable So as to get another free meal. Who are they lunching with?

Nora They're not exactly lunching. They went to a party last night.

Barnstable Oh I see. Not up yet.

By now Nora has tidied up the papers and taken them back to the table

Nora I shouldn't think they've been to bed. Apparently, these days parties go on till about four p.m. next day.

Barnstable watches her in complete silence, then rises, moves to the table, picks up the newspapers again, crosses back to the armchair, throws the papers down again and sits with one. Nora starts looking for something

Barnstable I like to know where they are. You did tell Roger that I particularly wanted to see him?

Nora No, dear.

Barnstable Why not?

Nora He might have thought you wanted to talk to him.

Barnstable Obviously.

Nora Then he wouldn't come. Roger knows when you talk to him you upset yourself. He is fond of you. He takes you seriously. I've explained there's no need, but I can't stop him. What did you want to talk to him about, this time?

Barnstable His career—and I don't mean in the Municipal Baths.

Nora He's very happy at the Municipal Baths. Why can't you leave him alone?

Barnstable I shall leave him alone, one of these days, but before that, I'd like to see him settled with some sort of future.

Nora He thinks he has a future as an author.

Barnstable If he spends all his time at the baths, when does he get any writing done? Underwater?

Nora In the evenings, I imagine.

Barnstable Then he could just as well come into the business. He'd still have his evenings free.

Nora (*on the floor*) He's not interested in fruit and vegetables.

Barnstable I don't sell fruit.

Nora It's the same thing. (*She puts the toy in the toy box and sits at the desk*)

Barnstable It's not the same thing at all. You always take his side.

Nora (*absently*) Yes, dear. (*She looks through various bills*)

Barnstable (*suddenly*) Roast chicken and queen's pudding!

Nora What did you say?

Barnstable For seventeen years we had roast chicken and queen's pudding for dinner every Sunday because Roger liked it. You never asked what I liked. I loathe roast chicken and queen's pudding.

Nora You should have said so sooner.

Barnstable It wouldn't have done any good, as long as Roger was around.

Nora We don't have it any more, dear. We have roast beef and apple tart, because that's what you like.

Barnstable Not when Roger comes. Then we go back to roast chicken and queen's pudding.

Nora He doesn't come often now, dear.

Barnstable I suppose that's my fault?

Nora Well, he's not like you. He doesn't like rows.

Barnstable I don't like rows!

Nora I daresay you don't, but you're always having them. It's as though you don't *want* to be happy.

Barnstable Of course I want to be happy! If only——

Nora (*kindly*) If only you weren't so tiresome, dear. Yes, I know.

Barnstable What would you say if I told you I only had a year to live?

Nora Have you been to the Army and Navy Stores lately?

Barnstable No.

Nora I don't understand why they've charged me for three bottles of whisky. You haven't sent whisky to anyone?

Barnstable No. You didn't answer my question.

Nora What was it, dear?

Barnstable What you'd do if I told you I had only a year to live?

Nora Is it a quiz?

Barnstable A quiz?

Nora Out of the *Sunday Express*?

Barnstable No.

Nora Your mother.

Barnstable What about her?

Nora She's always popping into the Army and Navy.

Barnstable What about it?

Nora They must have muddled the bills. Why should she buy three bottles of whisky? She hates whisky.

Barnstable It's absolutely extraordinary.

Nora I know, but that's what must have happened.

Barnstable It's absolutely extraordinary that you and I can never have a conversation. You never listen to anything I say. You're always doing something else. I suppose you don't want to talk to me.

Nora I don't mind talking to you, dear. But I'd rather talk about something sensible.

Barnstable The whisky bill.

Nora I can do something about a whisky bill. I can't do anything about your dying within a year.

Barnstable How would you feel about it?

Nora Sorry. I suppose Roger didn't find himself short and forgot to tell me?

Barnstable It doesn't matter.

Nora What doesn't matter?

Barnstable Three bottles of whisky don't matter, compared to what we're talking about.

Nora They matter very much to me. I don't like paying for things I didn't order. Nor do you.

Barnstable All right, then, I did order them.

Nora You said you didn't, just now.

Barnstable Now I say I did. I ordered them for the office party.

Nora Oh well that's different. I suppose it's deductible.

Barnstable Not any more.

Nora Then it's very extravagant. I thought office parties were going out.

Barnstable It's the last one I shall give.

Nora Good.

Barnstable You never came to one, did you?

Nora You never asked me.

Barnstable Most of the other wives came.

Nora If you like, I'll come next year.

Barnstable I've just said I'm not planning any more.

Nora Good.

Barnstable Perhaps you'd like to know why I'm not planning any more?

Nora I don't think so, dear, as long as you've decided. I expect it was the right decision. (*She begins to count on her fingers*)

Barnstable Very well, here it is. I've got a year to live. It's not a lot, but it will do me. Before you say anything, let's get one thing clear—I don't want any sympathy, and I don't want to discuss it. I don't see any point in telling Roger, and I certainly don't want Mother to know. Do you agree?

Nora (*who has not listened to a word*) Yes, dear.

Barnstable Very well then. I know this must be a shock for you. Don't say anything just now. Then when the shock wears off, we can discuss it calmly and make whatever arrangements have to be made. I tell you what—just now, let's pretend I haven't told you. (*He goes to her on a sudden impulse and kisses her*)

Nora Good-bye, dear.

Barnstable I'm not going just yet.

Nora (*opening her eyes, puzzled*) You're not?

Barnstable No. What are you thinking?

Nora I'm trying to remember when I last went to the Army and Navy Stores.

Barnstable (*impressed by such fortitude*) That's my girl.

Nora Do you want to come here?

Barnstable You've got guts. (*Caught up in amateur dramatics, he produces his wallet, extracts a tenner, and puts it in Nora's hand*)

Nora What's that for?

Barnstable For you. Shall we go to bed?

Nora (*startled*) Now?

Barnstable Yes, now.

Nora What on earth for?

Barnstable takes the tenner back, folds it up carefully and puts it back in his wallet.

Barnstable I bore you in bed, don't I?

Nora No, of course not. But we haven't been to bed for——

Barnstable Don't start working it out. I'm not the Army and Navy Stores.
You don't want to?
Nora Well of course I want to. But I think it's going to rain. I must get
the clothes off the line. And the children will be here in a minute.

Nora starts to go into the garden as Selena and Roger are heard off

There are the children. Do something, Henry.
Barnstable You called me Henry.
Nora What does it matter what I called you? You must know who you
are by this time, surely!

Nora exits to the garden
   Selena enters from the hall with some clothing, followed by Roger

Selena (*speaking as she enters*) I thought he might be useful to you. I tell
you he was a publisher.
Roger How could he be a publisher? He was wearing a dhoti.
Selena That's what publishers wear nowadays. Hullo, Pa.
Barnstable Hullo, Selena. I see you've brought the laundry.
Selena No, it's the dry-cleaning, actually. Roger's got the laundry. (*She
throws the clothes in a corner*)
Barnstable How's the glass-blowing?
Selena That was last term.
Barnstable Oh, really. What is it this term?
Selena I've started throwing pots.
Barnstable Hit anyone yet?
Selena Oh, Pa.
Roger Where's Adam?
Barnstable Taking your grandmother for a walk. (*Looking at their trendy
clothes*) I do wish you both wouldn't come here dressed like that. This
is a very nice neighbourhood. People pay a lot of money for houses
round here. They don't want to look out of their windows every Sunday
and say, "Oh my God, the gypsies are back".
Roger Well we're not trying to sell them clothes pegs, Pa.
Barnstable I wouldn't put it past you. I'm afraid you'll have to wait for
your tea. We didn't expect you so soon.
Selena Roger got bored as usual, so we left early.
Roger I didn't, it was you who wanted to push off.
Selena You looked bored as soon as the food ran out.
Roger I was fascinated by our hostess. She told me she was only really
happy in bed and wondered why she bothered to keep getting up.
Selena Did you offer to go to bed with her?
Roger She goes to bed to read eleventh-century French history. I found
her a rather elegant cow.

*As Barnstable is about to sit on the sofa, Roger puts his feet up. Selena is
occupying the armchair. Barnstable is reduced to the upright chair by the
desk*

Barnstable (*with heavy sarcasm*) Is this chair free, do you happen to know? (*He sits down*).

Selena Her husband was a drag. I never want to hear a zither played in the bath again.

Barnstable He played his zither in his bath?

Selena I've just said so, Pa.

Barnstable Did you watch?

Selena I didn't mind watching, it was having to listen.

Barnstable Do you usually watch men in their baths? I'm not criticizing, just asking for information.

Selena He was giving the party. One had to humour the guy.

Barnstable Roger, you should have interfered.

Roger Why, Pa?

Barnstable Exposing your wife to that sort of filth.

Roger She wasn't exposed, Pa. Nor was he exposed. He had his clothes on.

Barnstable In the bath? He was drunk?

Selena He didn't even get wet.

Barnstable Why not?

Roger There wasn't any water in the bath.

Selena He did it because he thought it sounded better that way. It's lateral thinking, Pa. Look, I'll give you another one. There were three worms crossing the road. Daddy Worm, Mummy Worm and Baby Worm. Baby Worm says, "Look, there are four of us crossing the road". Why?

Roger Baby Worm can't count.

Selena Right!

Barnstable Baby Worm can't count?

Nora enters from the garden with washing

Nora Hullo, we didn't expect you yet. Gran has taken Adam to the Park.

Selena You shouldn't have done all that washing. Here, let me take some. (*She goes to take some of the washing*)

Nora Oh, that's all right.

Nora and Selena both start to exit, talking as they go

I like to do it. We'll put it on the clothes-horse in the kitchen.

Barnstable Nora.

Nora Yes?

Barnstable There were three worms crossing the road. Daddy Worm, Mummy Worm and Baby Worm. Baby Worm says, "Look, there are four of us crossing the road." Why?

Nora Baby Worm can't count.

Barnstable in a fury scrumples up his newspaper

Nora and Selena exit

Barnstable (*to Roger*) How are the baths going? Plenty of clean towels?

Roger Yes, thank you. Why do you always ask idiot questions? I don't ask if you've squashed any good tomatoes lately.

Barnstable I'm just trying to take an interest in your career. There's not a great deal to take an interest in. Towels, water—I think I asked about the soap last time. Never mind. Plenty of soap?

Roger I wish I could get it into your head that the Municipal Baths is not a career.

Barnstable I've got that into my head.

Roger It's just a job. It could be any job. Who cares?

Barnstable Who *cares*? You spend two-thirds of your life doing it.

Roger *You* may. I don't intend to. As long as I can earn enough to live on.

Barnstable But you don't. You have half your meals here. You use your mother and your grandmother as unpaid baby-sitters. You turn this house every Sunday into a Chinese laundry and dry cleaning establishment.

Roger All right, if that's how you feel, we won't come here any more.

Barnstable You depend on me to go on working hard at my business so that you can spend a few hours a day handing out bath towels and the rest of the time enjoying yourself.

Roger I don't believe there's any particular merit in working from nine to five. What's the point of it?

Barnstable The point is to make a living, so that you can afford to get married and have a family and watch them grow up to throw it in your face.

Roger I'm not throwing it in your face. I'm trying to make you understand my point of view. Business is only a means to an end. The whole thing has got screwed up. The sensible ones are the ones who aren't in business.

Barnstable Municipal Bath attendants?

Roger Writers, painters, actors, the criminal classes.

Barnstable Have you thought what will happen to your mother when I'm dead?

Roger She'll be a widow. I'm sorry, Pa. What will happen to her?

Barnstable If the business closes down, what do you suppose she'll have to live on?

Roger By then, perhaps, I'll be selling my books.

Barnstable A year from now?

Roger Not as soon as that—you're not going to die in a year, are you?

Barnstable I am, as a matter of fact.

Roger What makes you think that?

Barnstable I'd like to show you some pictures.

Roger Don't change the subject, Pa.

Barnstable You never believe a word I say. These are the X-rays of a man who has about twelve months to live. They happen to be my X-rays.

Roger How do you know?

Barnstable I was there when they took them.

Roger I don't know what I'm looking at these for. They don't mean a thing to me. There must be something they can do.

Barnstable Nothing anyone can do. I'm afraid you must take my word for that too.

Roger I certainly won't take your word for that. What do they say is the matter with you?

Barnstable It's called Blum's Disease.

Roger I've never heard of it.

Barnstable That doesn't surprise me. It doesn't surprise me in the least.

Roger What's the name of your specialist? You went to one, I take it? This isn't Burrows' idea?

Barnstable I don't want to discuss it.

Roger We're going to discuss it, Father. For once, we are going to sit down and have a serious discussion. What's the name of your chap?

Barnstable I don't propose to tell you. Everyone agrees he's the expert.

Roger I don't.

Barnstable I'm sure he'll be very worried when he hears about that.

Roger I'm going to see to it you get another opinion. What about Switzerland or the States? There's always a top cat about if you look for him.

Barnstable I don't want to waste a lot of money chasing quacks.

Roger They're not quacks simply because they don't live in England.

Barnstable We won't argue about it. I didn't expect you to believe me. You've never believed anything I've told you.

Roger Don't start that again. Can't you see I'm trying to help?

Barnstable If you want to help, you can come into the business.

Roger For heaven's sake, Pa, don't go on about the bloody business. Can't you understand—(*shouting*)—it doesn't matter now?

Barnstable (*shouting*) NO, I CAN'T! (*Speaking quietly*) Don't raise your voice, Roger. I want this kept Top Secret.

Roger Top Secret? Aren't you going to tell Mother?

Barnstable I have told your Mother.

Roger How did she take it?

Barnstable She was magnificent. She didn't argue.

Roger Can I tell Selena?

Barnstable If you think she'd be interested.

Roger Pa!

Barnstable I don't propose to tell your grandmother and I must ask you not to do so.

Roger But why, Pa?

Barnstable Because, Roger, I happen to be her son, and being a son is something that I don't think you have ever quite understood.

Barnstable starts to exit to the garden

Roger Pa!

Barnstable (*coming back*) Yes?

Roger I'm terribly sorry.

Barnstable For whom?

Roger Well—for you.

Barnstable I'm sorry for you, Roger. Let's leave it at that, shall we?

As Barnstable exits through the window Selena enters from the hall

Selena Are you coming out?
Roger No, I don't think so.
Selena Have you got your toothache?

Roger shakes his head

Do you think that life is so absolutely glorious that you can hardly bear it?
Roger No, I don't think so.
Selena That's what I thought. (*She sits down and picks up a paper*)
Roger I thought you were going to meet Gran.
Selena I am. Do you want to hear your stars? "A new venture brings new responsibilities. Do not get carried away." Do you want to hear mine?
Roger No, thanks.
Selena Where's Pa?
Roger He's in the garden. He thinks he's going to die.
Selena (*laughing*) Honestly!
Roger Yes, honestly.
Selena Did he tell you that?
Roger Among other things.
Selena What other things?
Roger It doesn't matter.
Selena Is it true?
Roger He seemed to think so.
Selena What's he going to do about it?
Roger Die, I suppose. What can he do? He wants me to go into the business.
Selena What is it?
Roger Something called Blum's Disease. He showed me the X-rays. He seemed to be rather proud of them.
Selena Why?
Roger Why was he proud of them?
Selena Why did he show them to you?
Roger Proof, I suppose. You know he likes everything in black and white. Black and grey.
Selena Yes. Do you think it's a trick?
Roger A *trick*? That's an awful thing to say! Apart from anything else, he wouldn't have the imagination . . . (*He stops short*)
Selena He's always wanted you to go into the business. I can't imagine why. You'd be absolutely hopeless at it.
Roger No, I would not.
Selena Of course you would!
Roger Well, good God, there's nothing very difficult about selling fruit.
Selena He doesn't sell fruit, it's vegetables.
Roger It's the same thing. People do it off barrows all the time.

Selena But this is big business.

Roger It's exactly the same principle. I took charge of a stall of oranges once, in Berwick Street market.

Selena Did you sell any?

Roger No.

Selena That's what I mean.

Roger What the hell are we talking about bloody oranges for!

Selena Don't take out your guilt feelings on me.

Roger What guilt feelings?

Selena You never liked your father——

Roger I do like him!

Selena Go on! You don't even like him as much as I do.

Roger And God knows, that isn't much!

Selena Yes, it is. I like him quite a lot. He exasperates me, but I like him. Yes, that's the difference between us. He exasperates me more, but I like him better. And he exasperates you less, but you don't like him so much.

Roger (*shouting at the top of his voice*) *I like him!*

Selena (*very calmly*) All right, you like him. No need to get uptight over it.

Roger I thought you were going out for a walk.

Selena Changed my mind.

Roger (*going to the window*) He's still in the garden. He's looking at the roses. He's trying to pull the greenfly off the buds, but he always pulls the buds off as well. (*He moves away from the window and sits*) I really do like him.

Selena I know.

Roger You know what I like best about him? He's such a fighter. Life, to him, is one long, glorious battle. Everything he says to us is part of the fight—bath towels, your art, Adam's upbringing. And now, there's a battle that he can't win but comes out fighting just the same. I know it sounds terribly corny, but he really has got the courage of a lion. And no matter how much you hurt him, he never lets you know.

There is a scream from the garden and Barnstable comes charging into the room. He has taken off his jacket

Barnstable OOOWWW!!! Aw! Ow! God damn it, that hurts!

Roger What on earth's the matter?

Barnstable (*undoing his shirtsleeve*) I've been stung by a bee. Don't stand there, get me something. Roger! Selena! DO something!

Selena What do you want us to do?

Barnstable (*running to the door*) Nora, Nora, Nora! Where's your mother?

Roger She's ironing, Pa.

Barnstable Ask your mother for some tweezers . . .

Roger Tweezers?

Barnstable Tweezers! And get some blue bag.

Roger Blue bag!

Barnstable Blue bag, blue bag, blue bag! Haven't we got any blue bag?

Roger I'll go and see.

Roger exits to the hall

Barnstable Tell your mother I've been badly bitten by a bee.

Selena Let me look.

Barnstable It's no use your looking. I know what it is. It's a sting. I saw the brute—it crawled up my arm. There you are—that's the sting in the centre—that black thing.

Selena Here?

Barnstable Don't mess it about, for heaven's sake. Wait for the tweezers.

Selena I think I can squeeze it out.

Barnstable Ow! That hurt! Be careful.

Selena That's not a sting. It's just a thorn.

Barnstable It's the sting. Now you've taken the top off. We'll never find it. It's gone right in. You pushed it in.

Roger enters with a pair of tweezers

Roger Here you are, Pa. She says they're her eyebrow tweezers, so be careful with them.

Barnstable (*outraged*) Be careful with them? Where's the blue bag?

Roger Mother's looking for it.

Barnstable The whole point of blue bag is to put it on right away. If you've had to look for it, it's too late.

Selena (*taking the tweezers from him*) Now, Pa, give me the tweezers. Tell me exactly where you think the sting is.

Barnstable Where do you think? Where it's starting to swell up. That's what comes of messing about with it. Ow! Ow! I can't take much more of this. Roger, go and get a chemist.

Roger What do you want a chemist for?

Barnstable I don't want a chemist. I want something for blood poisoning. I don't want to lose my bloody hand!

Nora enters with a bottle and cotton-wool

Nora Did you say you'd been stung?

Barnstable I'm so glad the news has percolated at last.

Nora (*taking over from Selena*) Where is it?

Barnstable Here. Here! The sting is still in.

Nora I don't see any sting.

Selena Nor did I.

Barnstable Selena broke the head off. It's right in there, deep down. Look, I can't flex my finger now. It's stiffening up.

Nora Did you see the wasp?

Barnstable Wasp? It was a queen bee. I can feel the poison going all the way up my arm. I think I'm going to faint. (*He sits down*) I'd better put my head between my knees. (*He attempts it, but can't get down far enough*)

Nora Nonsense, Barney! Of course you're not going to faint. Now, let me put some of this on. (*She sits him in the armchair*)

Barnstable Haven't we got any blue bag?

Nora This is better than blue bag. More modern. It's anti-histamine.

Barnstable Blue bag draws out the sting.

Nora So does this. Hold still. Do you want a Bandaid on it?

Barnstable Well, I don't want to get any dirt in it.

Nora There's nothing to get dirt into. Still, if you want a Bandaid, you can have a Bandaid.

Barnstable It doesn't matter. Forget the Bandaid. If it's too much trouble to put a Bandaid on, just say so.

Nora Selena, go upstairs to the bathroom and get some Bandaids, will you.

Barnstable I don't want them! Forget the bloody Bandaid! Forget the whole bloody thing! So I've got a poisoned hand—all right, I'll have it off. (*Suddenly berserk*) You don't care what happens to me—you never cared, any of you. I'm bloody well dying and you can't even spare the time to bandage my hand!

Nora Dying? What on earth are you talking about?

Barnstable It's easy for you to keep calm. You don't care. Nobody cares. Henry doesn't care . . .

Roger Pa . . .

Barnstable You don't care. I ask one thing of you. I say, "Will you come into the business?" "No bloody fear", you say, "I don't want to." You drivel on, expounding your half-baked theories . . .

Roger I've changed my mind. I will come in.

Selena Roger . . .

Barnstable I don't want you, do you hear? I don't want you! I can do without you—(*to Nora*)—and you—(*to Selena*)—and I can certainly do without you. Baby Worm can't count!

Nora Barney, stop it! Do you hear? Stop it at once! Control yourself!

Barnstable Control myself? I've controlled myself all my life, and now, by God, I'm going to say what I think and do what I think and live my own life—what's left of it—and you can all go to hell!

At the height of the noise and fury, Mother enters

Mother What on earth is the matter? I can hear you shouting all down the road. You'll wake Adam.

Barnstable This is nothing to do with you, Mother. Keep out of it.

Nora He's just been telling us . . .

Barnstable Be quiet! I want my mother kept out of this. I've been stung, Mother, and . . .

Nora That's just what I was . . .

Barnstable Sh! I've been stung by a queen bee and I lost my temper. I don't want you to ask what the row was about because you're not going to be told, and we're not going to discuss it any more. Now, let's have some tea. I'll put the kettle on. There's nothing like a nice cup of tea.

Barnstable exits

Nora Has he gone mad? What's he talking about? He's not going to die from being stung by a bee.

Selena No, but he is going to die.

Mother Has he told you?

Roger He told me. And he said he'd told Mother.

Nora Told me what? You mean all that nonsense about having a poisoned hand?

Mother No, not that.

Roger Gran, he said he wasn't going to tell you.

Mother No, he didn't. But I talked to Dr Burrows and he told me at once.

Nora Told you what? What are you talking about?

Mother About Barney. It's just as he said. But you know that, dear. He is going to die.

Nora What? When?

Mother In about a year. Perhaps a little more.

Nora falls in a faint. When Nora is on the floor the others go to her

Barnstable enters

Barnstable Kettle's on. Won't be long now. (*Seeing Nora*) I'm not surprised. Who hit her?

CURTAIN

SCENE 2

The same. A month later

Henry is sitting with a document in his hand. Nora, Mother, Roger and Selena are ranged round him. Roger's hair is now cut short, and both he and Selena wear conventional clothes. Henry is reading from the document, Barnstable's will

Henry ". . . and I further bequeath to my son, Roger, any or all of my pictures that he may choose, my silver cigarette-case, my travelling clock, my cellar; all books whatsoever obtained by me, subject only to a proviso that if my widow should desire to retain any or all of the said pictures and books during her life-time, she is at liberty to do so . . ."

Roger (*interrupting*) Cellar? What cellar? We haven't even got a basement.

Mother No, dear, he means that "make-it-yourself" wine kit in the garage.

Nora Sh-sh! Don't interrupt.

Henry "Subject to the disposal of all my properties herein enumerated I

give, bequeath and appoint all my property whatsoever and whereso-
ever——

*Barnstable enters from the garden, rather casually dressed, with a knotted
scarf and open-necked shirt. Smiling happily, he saunters round behind the
group*

*While Henry continues reading, Barnstable walks behind sofa and stands
behind him on cue*

—including any property funds over which I have any power of appoint-
ment, unto my Trustee upon trust, to pay my funeral debts and testa-
mentary expenses and stand possessed of the net proceeds of sale
calling in or conversion into money of all parts of my estate remaining
uncoverted hereinafter collectively called my *resi*duary estate . . ."
Barnstable Residual.
Henry "Residual estate upon trust for my wife the said Nora Evange-
line . . ." (*Realizing that Barnstable has joined them*) Perhaps you'd like
to read it.
Barnstable No, no, you're reading it quite beautifully, Henry. I just
thought I'd mention it's "*resi*dual". That's what rehearsals are for—to
correct mistakes.
Henry I think we've rehearsed enough.
Barnstable There's a rather good bit coming—a sort of testament of faith
—I'd like you to hear.
Henry Well, we will hear it, old chap.
Barnstable When?
Roger When the time comes, Father.
Barnstable You mean when I'm dead? But I wanted to hear it.
Mother He wants to hear how it sounds. (*To Barnstable*) Why don't you
read it to us, dear?
Barnstable Well, of course, if it's too much trouble for my executor . . .
Henry No, no, it's just that I find it rather off-putting, your tiptoeing
round like a ghost. Perhaps if you went out of the room . . .
Barnstable Then I wouldn't hear it.
Nora You could sit outside the door . . .
Mother And if Henry spoke up . . .
Barnstable Why should I sit outside the door? It's my will. I want to
make sure it's all right.
Mother Indulge him, Henry.
Nora Yes, do, Henry. Come on, Barney. (*She picks up a box of chocolates*)
Come and sit by me. (*She moves along the sofa*) And have a chocky.

*Barnstable moves to her, takes the box of chocolates from her and offers
them to Henry, who starts to take one*

Henry No, thank you; not when I'm on duty. I've lost the place.
Barnstable I'll find it for you. I'm fairly familiar with the document. Here
you are.

Henry All right. But no more interruptions.
Barnstable (*sitting*) Certainly not.

Henry prepares to read

Take your time. It needs to be spaced out a bit. That's the way it's written. Get the cadence.

Henry takes a deep breath, manages to find a smile, and begins again

Henry "If she shall survive me for the period of one calendar month, but if my wife shall pre-decease me or not survive . . ."
Nora What, dear?
Barnstable I put that in in case of a car crash. In case we were both killed in a car.
Mother Very wise, dear, the way you drive.
Henry I've lost the thread. I really can't wade through all this.
Barnstable Come on, Henry, you've got to the last paragraph. That's the best part.
Henry (*throwing him a doubtful look*) Well . . .
Nora Go on, Henry.
Henry I wish everyone would stop saying "Go on, Henry"! I feel like a balky horse.
Barnstable You look like a balky horse! (*He laughs*)
Henry "Further to my last will and testament, I would like to thank all those members of my family and my friends, particularly my dear friend, Henry Poole——"
Mother There, that was worth waiting for, wasn't it?
Henry "—for all the help and encouragement they have given me during these last wonderful months . . ."
Nora What last wonderful months?
Barnstable Just looking ahead.
Roger I hope we can live up to it.
Barnstable I'm sure you will. Go on, Henry. Sorry.
Henry "—and I would like to put on record my gratitude particularly to my wife——"
Nora Oh, Barney!
Henry (*plodding again*) "—and to my son, Roger, for the way they have complied with my wishes, and for the sacrifice that the latter has made in giving up his promising career at the Municipal Baths and entering my business."
Selena Bloody hell!
Roger That's what I'm doing, aren't I?
Selena You needn't have put it in the will! Talk about moral blackmail! Anyway, he's a poet.
Barnstable I've made provision for that, later. Did you want to be in the will? I'm sorry, Selena, I could add a codicil.
Selena Please don't bother.
Roger Selena! Thank you, Pa. It was a very nice thought. And I'm sure Selena would like to be in the will. She's just a little shy.

Nora Go on, Henry. Sorry

Henry "I would like my funeral to be of the simplest——" I thought we'd dealt with the funeral.

Barnstable I've changed it.

Henry Oh. "I direct that my widow shall set aside the sum of twenty-five pounds out of my estate to pay for refreshments after the interment . . ."

Barnstable I decided you were right. A party would be nice.

Henry Twenty-five pounds?

Barnstable You think it's too much?

Henry "I wish to be laid to rest in a country churchyard . . ." I thought you wanted to be buried at sea.

Mother Oh no, dear. Not in Conservation Year.

Barnstable I thought you'd like a headstone.

Nora What would I do with it?

Barnstable You could share it later. Lower down.

Henry "I would like a plain headstone of Portland Stone or marble, not composition . . ."

Barnstable I feel quite strongly about that.

Selena Quite right, Pa.

Mother I'm not sure you'd like marble.

Barnstable Why not?

Mother So cold.

Barnstable I'm not going to sit on it, Mother.

Mother Very wise, dear. Go on, Henry. (*She looks at him, hesitates and decides not to apologize*)

Henry "—and on it to be simply inscribed an epitaph of not more than four lines. I would like the lines to rhyme——"

Roger Oh, Pa! No!

Barnstable Wait for it.

Henry "—and to be composed by my son, Roger."

Barnstable And I don't want a limerick.

Roger glances, dismayed, at Selena

Henry folds the will up

Henry Thank God that's settled.

Barnstable Just a moment. I should like the refreshments to consist of champagne, to be served in magnums.

Henry For twenty-five pounds it'll be served in splits!

Barnstable I shall add a codicil to that effect.

Henry If you add a codicil, I must decline to act as your executor.

Nora Henry, that's rather unkind.

Henry Not at all. As far as I'm concerned, this will has become an absolute bloody menace. The whole thing's thoroughly morbid.

Barnstable Morbid? There's nothing morbid about it. Quite the opposite. I want you all to familiarize yourselves with the document so that when the time comes it will not be such a shock.

Henry It's hardly likely. We've heard it three times already.

Barnstable Up to now we've only heard the rough drafts. This is the finished article.

Henry I sincerely hope so.

Mother It's a very nice will, dear, and I'm sure we'll all enjoy it when the time comes. Now, you've had quite enough chocolates for today; you'll make yourself ill.

Mother takes the box of chocolates and exits through the dining-room

Selena Can I help with the washing-up, Mother?

Nora No, I can manage, dear. You take Adam for his walk.

Nora exits to the hall

Selena Rog, come and get the pram round.

Roger O.K.

Selena You coming with us?

Roger No. I must go to the office.

Selena You can't go to the office today. It's Sunday.

Roger People work on Sundays. Henry does.

Henry (*still holding the will*) Where there's a Will there's a lot of hard work.

Roger I want to plan a new campaign for beetroots. The office is quiet on a Sunday.

Selena So is a funeral parlour.

Roger What's that supposed to mean?

Selena As far as Adam and I are concerned, for the past week, you might as well have been dead. No offence, Pa.

Barnstable Of course not. I never believed I had the monopoly.

Roger I happen to have been busy.

Selena You happen not to have seen your son for a week, except when he's asleep. It makes him feel very insecure.

Roger He shouldn't feel insecure. I've just paid his first educational premium.

Selena Pity you haven't told him. You sound more like your father every day!

Selena bangs out to the hall

Barnstable Fancy, a compliment from Selena!

Roger Yes. See you, Pa.

Barnstable I hope so, indeed.

Roger exits to the hall. Mother enters from the dining-room

Mother I've left my glasses somewhere. Have you seen them, Barney?

Barnstable (*rising*) No. (*He starts to exit to the dining-room*)

Mother I didn't leave them in the dining-room, Barney, if that's where you're going to look.

Barnstable I didn't suppose you did, Mother. I'm just going to take a leak.

Mother Barney, I do wish you wouldn't discuss it. Just go away and do it quietly, dear.

Barnstable I do do it quietly, Mother. But somehow these social conventions don't seem to matter as much as they did.

Barnstable exits

Henry The old boy's doing jolly well.

Mother (*hunting under cushions and on tables*) As long as he concentrates on death he'll be fine. I just hope he doesn't start thinking about life.

Henry You think that would be a mistake?

Mother He might realize what he's missed.

Henry I don't think he's missed all that much.

Mother is still turning over cushions

Mother He always wanted to be captain of his side. He never even got picked for the team. In the end, he gave up the game. Now, of course, he's become the guest of honour. That's what he always wanted. To be the child who goes up on the stage and helps the conjuror.

Barnstable enters with Mother's glasses

Barnstable Here you are, Mother. That's where they were. Two birds with one stone. You must have taken them off when you sat down.

Mother exits to the hall, taking the glasses

Talking about birds, Henry, you remember you were going to find me one?

Henry I made a few inquiries without much success, I'm afraid. The trouble is, I don't fancy myself in the role of a ponce. If you want a final fling, as you call it, couldn't you make your own arrangements?

Barnstable It would be less trouble if you made them, old friend. I don't quite know where to look.

Henry What about your friendly neighbourhood newsagent.

Barnstable Newsagent?

Henry Hasn't he got a board in the window?

Barnstable What sort of board?

Henry I know you said that sex is a secret society, but it's not quite as secret as it used to be. You will find, if you care to take a stroll down the Earls Court Road, for instance, all sorts of suggestions pinned to doorways or displayed in windows.

Barnstable What suggestions?

Henry "Modern Dancing Taught in Strict Tempo."

Barnstable I don't want to learn dancing.

Henry You may not have to, but you might find the answer to your problem.

Barnstable I'd much rather you did it, old man. You're supposed to be my executor.

Henry Barney, my duties as executor don't start until you're dead.

Barnstable I think you ought to get some practice, first. The way things are going, I don't think I'll even get buried.

Henry Strictly speaking, that's the undertaker's job, but I'll see you get buried. It'll be a damned sight easier than this. At least you won't be there interfering.

Barnstable That was in rather bad taste. Not very accurate, either.

Henry Well, you will be there, but you won't be interfering—will you?

Barnstable No, I'll make damned sure it's all planned beforehand. We ought to choose the cemetery.

Henry I thought we had.

Barnstable I hear there's a very pretty one at Stoke Poges.

Henry Stoke Poges? You've gone off Marlow, then?

Barnstable I haven't gone off it, but it looks rather full, and I have an idea it's damp. I took Nora down there for lunch on Thursday. Didn't tell her why, of course.

Henry Just wandered round the cemetery with her? It must have made a nice outing.

Barnstable It did, rather. We had a little picnic on the gravestones. She made the most delicious sandwiches. Stoke Poges is nearer. Perhaps you'd like to pop down there with me some time and, if we like it, we'll site the grave.

Henry Not much.

Barnstable I think it will interest you, Henry. It's where the ploughman is buried, you know.

Henry What ploughman?

Barnstable Gray's ploughman. "Homeward the ploughman plods his weary way, and leaves the world to darkness and to me."

Henry He isn't buried there.

Barnstable Yes, he is. That's the whole point.

Henry "Homeward the ploughman plods his weary way."

Barnstable That's right. I learnt it at school. It's stuck in my mind.

Henry I don't care where it's stuck. He wasn't dead. He was going home to tea.

Barnstable He's dead.

Henry By now, he's certainly dead. He wasn't dead then. Gray saw him going home.

Barnstable It's an elegy written in a churchyard.

Henry But not an epitaph.

Barnstable It's the same thing. It's what you say over people when they're dead.

Henry Barney, that is a eulogy.

Barnstable They spelt it differently in those days.

Henry And anyway, if he was buried there, how could he keep on plodding home? This is the most ridiculous conversation I've ever had.

Barnstable I don't have to explain the poem to you. You're supposed to

be the literary editor. How would you like a series of articles for your
paper?
Henry (*off guard*) What about?
Barnstable Having only a year to live.
Henry Oh.
Barnstable I thought I'd call them, "Hail, Caesar". Rather good?
Henry Inspired.
Barnstable You know the quotation?
Henry Yes, indeed. Will my readers?
Barnstable Henry, I'm pretty sure if you knew it, most of your readers
would.

Henry gives Barney the will

What do you want me to do with this?
Henry Have it signed and witnessed.
Barnstable Well, that's easy. Don't go away, Henry. I'll sign it and you
witness it.
Henry (*shaking his head*) I'm your executor. You need two independent
witnesses.
Barnstable Justices of the Peace?
Henry No, ordinary people.
Barnstable Passers-by?
Henry Yes, I suppose so.
Barnstable Right, then. Off you go.
Henry Where?
Barnstable To the gate. Acting as my executor to get the first two people
passing by to act as witness to my will.
Henry Well, I can hardly drag two people in off the street.
Barnstable Why not?
Henry They wouldn't come.
Barnstable Want to bet?
Henry I suppose if you stood at the gate long enough, you'd eventually
find two cranks whose lifetime's ambition it was to witness somebody's
will, but . . .
Barnstable Not eventually. The first two who come along.
Henry The bet is, the first two people who pass will be eager to be witnesses.
Barnstable Not eager. Prepared.
Henry How much do you want to bet?
Barnstable I don't mind—five quid?
Henry Make it ten.
Barnstable Ten. All right. You wait here.
Henry Not on your life.
Barnstable You don't trust me?
Henry On a bet like this, certainly not.
Barnstable Perhaps you'd rather go?
Henry Much rather.
Barnstable If you're not prepared to trust me, I don't see why I should
trust you.

Henry We'll both go.

Barnstable Two people might put them off. They might think they're going to be coshed!

Roger enters with bowler, umbrella and briefcase

Roger Henry, are you going to your office? I thought you might drop me off at mine.

Barnstable and Henry look at each other

Barnstable He'll do.

Roger Do what?

Barnstable Just go down to the gate, will you, Roger, and ask the first two people who pass if they'll step in here for a moment?

Roger What for?

Henry We want them to witness your father's will.

Barnstable You don't have to tell them, at this stage.

Henry Oh yes, you do.

Roger Do you mean perfect strangers?

Henry Yes. (*Taking Roger's bowler, briefcase and umbrella*) Don't look too formal.

Barnstable It doesn't matter if you know them. That'll be the luck of the draw. The point is that they must be adults—two consenting adults. I wouldn't have made that joke a month ago!

Henry Pity you made it now!

Barnstable Roger, ask them to come into your Father's house—— No, don't put it like that. They'll think he's a religious maniac. We just want their signatures.

Roger I don't think they'll agree for a moment.

Barnstable Of course they will. One thing I've learnt since I've been ill is how helpful everyone is. Don't be defeatist about it. Bring 'em back. Preferably alive. There's money involved.

Roger What do you mean, there's money involved?

Barnstable We've made a bet. Five pounds.

Henry Ten.

Roger I really think you'd do better to go yourself, Pa.

Barnstable Please, Roger, it's not a thing I'm going to ask you to do very often—to witness your old father's will.

Roger Well, if you put it like that——

Barnstable Good.

Roger sets off for the door

Bring the first one back and then get the other one. We don't want them hanging around.

Roger exits to the hall

Henry I can't say I envy him.

Barnstable Nonsense. (*Putting his photograph on the coffee table*) Give me the will, Henry. The blotter, and the pen.

Henry (*giving the blotter and pen to Barnstable*) What are you doing now?

Barnstable I'm getting ready for the will-signing ceremony. Do we need a Bible? (*He sets the will and writing materials on the coffee table*)

Henry What for?

Barnstable Do they have to swear? (*He arranges a bowl of flowers around the set-up, sticking some into his photograph*)

Henry I don't think they have to, but I'm pretty certain they will—being dragged off the streets! I don't think flower arranging is quite your thing. Anyway, why do you have artificial flowers?

Barnstable It's Mother. She can't bear picking real flowers. She says she can hear them scream. She's a member of SAFA.

Henry Dare I ask what SAFA is?

Barnstable It's the Society of Artificial Flower Arrangers.

Henry How about a drink?

Barnstable Do you think they'll expect one?

Henry I don't know about them; I'm expecting one. (*He goes to the drinks table*)

Barnstable Now for the stakes. (*Taking out a ten pound note*) Come on, Henry. Money on the table.

Henry Do you think that's wise? (*He takes out a note*)

Barnstable Certainly.

Henry In the unlikely event of Roger finding two lunatic hooligans, we don't know who they'll be.

Barnstable Well?

Henry I think it would be much better if we put them to bed in here. (*He puts them in a desk drawer, then sits*) We should have put a time limit on this bet.

Barnstable Getting cold feet?

Henry Of course not. The bet was the first two who passed. Someone must have passed by now.

Barnstable Not on a Sunday. Very quiet around here on a Sunday. (*Pause*) Isn't it exciting?

Henry I really ought to be at the office.

Barnstable Henry, it's extraordinary that you don't seem to enjoy anything any more. I should have thought that being my executor would have given you a new lease of life. You seem so listless. You don't care about choosing the grave. You don't take any interest in the will-signing. You haven't even taken the first step towards finding me a bird.

Poppy enters with Roger

Henry Roger, we'll need two of them.

A Police Constable enters

Constable What's all this then?

Barnstable Good afternoon, Constable. Very good of you to co-operate.

Constable I don't know about that, sir. This gentleman claims to be your son.

Poppy That's typical, isn't it?

Roger Is it?

Poppy Twisting things. "*Claims* to be his son."

Roger I am his son.

Poppy That's got nothing to do with it.

Roger Oh, hasn't it?

Constable I'll ask the questions, if you don't mind.

Barnstable No, I'll ask the questions. Can I have your name, rank and number?

Constable I was about to ask you your name, sir.

Barnstable Why, do you want your will witnessed? I want you to witness my will.

Constable I can't do that, sir. I'm on duty.

Barnstable If you're not prepared to co-operate, I don't know why you came in here.

Constable I came in here, sir, because this gentleman, who you say is your son . . .

Barnstable I didn't say he was my son.

Constable Ah. (*He starts to get out his notebook*)

Barnstable But as a matter of fact, he is.

The Constable eyes him severely

Constable He was loitering in the drive, and he accosted this young woman . . .

Roger I didn't accost her.

Poppy You said, "Oi!"

Roger Exactly.

Constable He then took this young woman by the arm and dragged her into the house.

Henry He wasn't supposed to drag her. That means I've won the bet.

Constable Bet?

Barnstable I just want my will witnessed.

Constable I may have to make out a report.

Roger What on earth for?

Constable Harassing a police officer in the course of his patrol.

Barnstable Surely it is your duty to assist the public? We are the public and we are asking for your assistance. What's wrong with that?

Constable Frivolous. It was a frivolous request.

Barnstable Frivolous? Of course it isn't frivolous. There's nothing frivolous about witnessing a will. Supposing I told you I was dying?

Constable You don't look to me as though you're dying.

Barnstable Well, that's just where you're wrong, because I am. That's why I want my will witnessed.

Constable I'd want proof of that, sir.

Barnstable Would you like to see my X-rays?

Constable That's up to you, sir.
Barnstable (*as he goes to the bookshelves to get them, to Henry*) They're
simply not getting the type of man they need in the force these days.
Roger It's perfectly true, Constable, he is going to die.
Constable Well, that does put a different complexion on the matter,
though I must say it seems a funny way of going about it. (*To Henry*)
Do you know anything about this, sir?
Henry No. I just dropped in to deliver a telegram.
Barnstable Henry! Come and help me! I've lost the X-rays.

*Henry goes to Barnstable, who takes several volumes down and they both
start to look through them*

Constable Now, if I might have your names.
Roger What for?
Constable I have to report the incident, sir.
Roger What incident?
Poppy He wants an incident. Let's give him one. (*She slaps the Constable's
face*) You can report that for a start.
Constable All right, we'll start with you. What's your name?
Poppy I don't want to give you my name.
Constable One of those, eh? (*He slaps Poppy's face*)

Barnstable and Henry drop downstage with books in their arms

Roger What the hell do you think you're doing?
Constable I don't like being hit about the face by members of the public,
and perhaps this young lady will think twice, now, before she hits
another policeman. Far too many young people, nowadays, think that
they have the right to assault the . . .
Poppy Pigs!
Constable Well, they haven't. What they have is a duty to assist us, and
that's something they forget, with all their other duties.
Roger Well, I still think . . .
Constable I shouldn't, sir.
Roger What?
Constable Think. You all think you're very smart, don't you, amusing
yourselves on a Sunday afternoon at the expense of the police force. (*To
Barnstable*) I don't include you, sir. If what you say is true, you have my
sympathy. None of us cares to face death—although the way things are
going in the world, a good many of us will probably be facing it sooner
than we expect. Poor consolation, sir, I know, but there it is. Not my
job to offer consolation, but it is my job to speak out when I'm slapped
in the face by a young lady of twenty-five dressed as a boy of twelve, for
no other reason than that I'm doing my duty as I see it. If you want to
report me, sir, my name is P.C. Stubbs, two-eight-six, Metropolitan
Division. In some ways it would be a relief if you would report me.
Might even get my discharge. It's a lousy job. Good afternoon, sir.

The Constable exits

Poppy Bloody Fascist!

Henry Oh, come, come, come, come! (*Giving his books to Barnstable*) Have a hernia to go with your Blum's Disease. Now, what was all that about? (*He replaces the books on the desk*)

Poppy What do you mean, he hit me, didn't he?

Henry You hit him first.

Poppy What's that got to do with it?

Henry (*unable to think of an answer, to Barney*) Well, I'm sorry, but I can't help you any more. Could I have my tenner?

Barney hands Henry one ten-pound note

I recognize this one. Can I have yours?

Barnstable The bet is void.

Henry Of course it isn't void. It's lost as far as you're concerned. He refused to witness your will. Are you refusing to pay your gambling debts?

Barnstable Certainly not. The bet is void.

Henry Very well, I shall take it out of the estate.

Barnstable Over my dead body.

Henry Probably. (*He goes to the door*)

Roger You haven't forgotten my lift, have you?

Henry No, no. How about you, old girl?

Poppy How about me?

Henry Can we give you a lift?

Poppy No, thanks.

Henry Do you hit many policemen?

Poppy Whenever I get the chance.

Henry Why?

Poppy Why not?

Henry I find people like you rather disquieting.

Poppy It's mutual.

Henry Is it? Well, good-bye. By the way, Barney, it's "E" for Enema.

Barnstable What's "E" for Enema.

Henry That's where you put the X-rays. See you later in the week, I expect. Possibly at Stoke Poges. If you get there first, start digging.

Henry exits

Roger looks doubtfully at Poppy, who is sitting on the sofa in the "lotus" position

Roger Will you be all right, Pa?

Barnstable I imagine so.

Roger Oh. 'Bye, then.

Roger goes to the desk to pick up his hat, umbrella and briefcase

Barnstable (*suddenly seeing Poppy*) You feeling all right?

Poppy Fine, thanks. Hey, do you still want me to witness your will?

Barnstable I don't think there's much point, now. You lost me my bet. *(He dismantles the coffee table, replacing the flowers and photograph)*
Poppy Bet?
Barnstable Yes. I think he would have witnessed it if you hadn't hit him. Why did you hit him like that? *(He puts the will away)*
Poppy Because he wanted to hit me. Well, one of us. I gave him the break he needed. The fuzz get very frustrated if they're not allowed to break out now and then. I'm a cathartic. I release people's hostility.
Barnstable I suppose I should feel hostile towards you; you cost me ten pounds. Somehow, I don't.
Poppy Well done.
Barnstable Can I offer you a cup of tea?
Poppy No, I don't think so, thanks. I've just had breakfast.

Barnstable looks at his watch, startled

Barnstable My name is Cuthbert Barnstable.
Poppy Never mind.
Barnstable What's yours?
Poppy Poppy.
Barnstable Poppy what?
Poppy Poppy—Seed! Does it matter?
Barnstable No.
Poppy Good. I travel light. Are you really going to die?
Barnstable Yes.
Poppy That's a bit of a drag.
Barnstable Yes, it is rather.
Poppy What are you going to do?
Barnstable Well, there's not a lot I can do. Except make arrangements.
Poppy What arrangements?
Barnstable Well, I've always liked everything cut and dried. That's why I was anxious to get my will witnessed. And then, of course, there's the grave to plan.
Poppy You're going to die at once, then?
Barnstable Not at once, no. A year. Eighteen months.
Poppy You mean you've got a whole year? Then what are you doing messing about with graves?
Barnstable What would you do?
Poppy Well, I certainly wouldn't spend the whole year in dying. What a waste! You could do that in a minute.
Barnstable Yes, I suppose I could. So what would you do instead?
Poppy I'd live. Do all the things I'd always wanted to do. If it was me, you know where I'd go? I'd go to Cuba.
Barnstable You're a Communist?
Poppy No, not particularly. But Cuba's a symbol. You should always go and look at symbols. There aren't many left.
Barnstable I've always wanted to go to Bognor Regis. Bognor Regis is a symbol to me.

Poppy I should go there, then. I'll go with you, if you like. Why don't we go this afternoon? We could hitch-hike.

Barnstable I have a car.

Poppy Then what we waiting for? Do the things you want to do. Then it'll be a gas instead of a drag.

Barnstable You know what I'd really like to do this afternoon?

Poppy What?

Barnstable No, perhaps not.

Poppy Perhaps not what?

Barnstable It's not the sort of thing one can just say right out.

Poppy What isn't?

Barnstable I doubt if Henry would even say it right out to Martha Hackney. Perhaps he would.

Poppy Say what?

Barnstable What I'd really like to do this afternoon is . . .

Poppy Yes?

Barnstable I find you most attractive. What I'd really like to do this afternoon is . . .

Poppy Go to bed?

Barnstable Yes! Could we?

Poppy Of course. (*She starts to strip off*) Easier than Bognor Regis.

Barnstable Not here!

Poppy No?

Barnstable My wife might come in.

Poppy You've got a wife?

Barnstable You've just met my son.

Poppy Yes, but I didn't know you'd got a wife as well.

Barnstable No, I suppose not.

Poppy Perhaps we'd better go to Bognor Regis after all.

Barnstable Yes, that would be best. Perhaps we could stop on the way?

Poppy My place?

Barnstable Could we?

Poppy Of course. (*Getting dressed again*) I shouldn't really be doing this.

Barnstable Not even Bognor Regis?

Poppy Not really. I should be at a rally to support the Young Gay Youth Movement. We were meeting at the Methodist Hall in Wright's Lane. That's off Kensington High Street. Then march on Somerset House. You see, if your sex is stated on your birth certificate you have to live out a pre-destined role and that's all wrong. Oh well—(*heading for the door*)—they'll just have to manage without me.

Barnstable It's such a lovely day. Shall we go through the garden?

Poppy looks at him. They both head towards the garden

Poppy Can I drive?

Mother enters

Barnstable Yes, of course. Miss Seed—we might have some difficulty starting. I'm afraid my battery could be a bit flat.

Mother Really, Barney, you should attend to your battery before you set out. Who's this?

Barnstable This is the young man from the garage, Mother. After you, Mr Seed.

CURTAIN

ACT II

Scene 1

The same. Eight months later

The living-room is in considerable disarray. The dining-room recess now has an erotic mural. A longbow and a sheaf of arrows are propped in a corner. Several model boats stand on a corner cupboard. A small Buddha in another corner has an offering of artificial flowers and joss-sticks. The bookcase is now a wine-rack filled with bottles. There is a bat in a cage, draped with a cloth

As the Curtain *rises, Henry and Barnstable enter from the double doors, carrying a low dining-table, which they place below the sofa. Barnstable wears a flashy pink suit*

Barnstable What d'you think of that, then? (*He indicates the table*)
Henry I'm sure it'll wash off.
Barnstable Henry, I've just painted it.

Barnstable goes back to the dining-room

Henry Sorry. By Jove!

Henry picks up the bow and fits an arrow to the string. He then sees a roller skate in the middle of the floor so stands on it while aiming the bow and arrow

Barnstaple enters with place mats, glasses and cutlery, and starts to lay the table

Oh, we going to have a picnic?
Barnstable It's a bistro-style. We're having bouillabaisse. Today, we visit the Camargue. I thought we'd have a month of French provincial cooking and then, perhaps, come a bit nearer home.
Henry By Jove! (*He wanders to a canvas and studies it*) By Jove!
Barnstable Why do you keep saying that?
Henry I never know what to say when I'm whipping round art centres.
Barnstable (*indicating the painting*) That's Mother. You've never studied art.
Henry I've studied your mother.
Barnstable (*bringing two more canvases forward*) You should take a course in appreciation, at least. Now then, these are two of my latest. This one is called, "Portrait of the Artist's Wife".

Henry Have you shown it to her?
Barnstable She sat for it. (*Putting second one on top*) You owe it to yourself. This one's called "Poppy's".
Henry Did she sit for you?
Barnstable More or less—you don't remember her?
Henry No.
Barnstable She was a witness.
Henry A Jehovah's Witness? By Jove! They are looking up.
Barnstable That's a trick of the light. It's funny to think a few months ago I knew as little about art as you do now. (*Seeing the cage*) Ah! You haven't met Vincent. (*He uncovers the bat*)
Henry Who's Vincent?
Barnstable Vincent Price. My bat. He's such a dear little chap. I got him last week. (*He starts to open the cage*)
Henry You're not going to let him out?
Barnstable I let him fly round once in a while. Why?
Henry Aren't they supposed to get in your hair?
Barnstable Well he won't stay long in yours. They have their own language, you know. Not just mating calls, but a perfectly understandable language.
Henry What's he saying now?
Barnstable He doesn't talk in his sleep. Give us your hand, Henry.
Henry Why?
Barnstable Let him hang on to you, for a bit. I'll give him his lunch. Now, don't be a coward, Henry. Mind he doesn't wake up. He could be hungry and give you a nip.
Henry What do you feed him on?
Barnstable Blood. He's a vampire bat.

Barnstable exits to the hall

Henry is aghast. He turns up his collar, looks round the room, tries to get the bat back into the cage, without success. He goes to the window, "throws" the bat away, but when he looks down it is still there! He tries again

Nora enters with a tray of glasses which she puts on the low dining-table

Nora What are you doing with Vincent?
Henry I couldn't get him back in his cage. Wing span.

Nora rather pityingly, takes the bat, opens the whole cage at base and casually throws the bat in the bottom

Nora (*taking the entire cage off to the dining-room*) I think he's had enough excitement for one day. (*As she re-enters*) Did he tell you about his new boat?
Henry Not yet.
Nora He's so excited about it. It came from America. It cost him a fortune. He's going to launch it this afternoon.

Henry Where?

Nora On the Round Pond. We're taking champagne. Are you coming?

Henry I doubt if I'll be up to it. Do you think he's gone off his head?

Nora No, of course not. He's just trying to make up for lost time. (*Picking up two canvases from the sofa where Barney left them, and indicating her own picture*) Doesn't that one remind you of Picasso?

Henry I never met him. Tell me, what's this sudden thing about bats?

Nora A talk he listened to on the radio.   .

Henry Like the bull-fighting?

Nora We're still hoping to go to Pamplona. He's so looking forward to running with the bulls.

Henry Actually, he's meant to run slightly ahead of them.

Nora Then you must tell him.

Henry I expect he'll find out.

Barnstable enters with bottle of wine in a cradle, and a container of blood

Barnstable Henry, I want your opinion on this. See if you can guess the Provenance. (*He pours wine*) Where's Vincent?

Nora I put him in the play-room.

Barnstable I'll just give him his lunch. Are you a blood-donor, Henry?

Barnstable exits to the dining-room

Henry nearly chokes on his wine, then nips over to look at the wine label. He moves away again as Barnstable speaks

(*off*) Well?

Barnstable enters

Henry It's a tricky one.

Barnstable Yes. Yes, it is. (*He is delighted that it is a challenge*)

Henry Well, it's a burgundy.

Barnstable You'll have to do better than that, Henry.

Henry *Château de Fleurie.*

Barnstable (*beginning to be unhappy*) Perhaps.

Henry (*sipping again*) Bottled in Beaune——

Barnstable Yes.

Henry —by Jean Larou—it's a guess, and only a guess, mind, I'd say the year was sixty-four. Back end.

Barnstable (*looking at Henry in astonishment*) I suppose that's an acceptable margin of error.

Mother enters with a dish of yoghourt and a spoon

Barnstable Why is it, Mother, that every time I cook, you decide it's your day for yoghourt?

Mother I don't decide. It says so on the carton.

Barnstable Says what?

Mother That it should be eaten today. (*She sits by the drinks cabinet and eats*)

Barnstable You shouldn't believe everything you read.

Mother I do on food cartons. They have to tell the truth or they're prosecuted. They're not like the newspapers.

Barnstable Really, Mother!

Barnstable exits to the hall

Henry Can't you persuade Barney to let you do the cooking?

Nora Not a hope. He's writing a cookery book.

Henry He shouldn't write one! He should read one!

Mother If the bouillabaisse isn't eatable, you shouldn't try and eat it. Tell him outright that he can't cook. He'll accept the truth if you're firm enough, and it won't upset him any more than it did when he was a little boy.

Henry Did he think he could cook when he was a little boy?

Mother He wanted everyone else to think he could cook. He couldn't bear to think people weren't going to notice him. Nobody did. He's not a very noticeable person.

Nora I noticed him.

Mother You married him, dear. It's not quite the same thing. Although I'm sure it made up for a lot of his disappointment.

Henry What's he got to be disappointed about?

Mother Nothing, now. That's what's so strange.

Nora He's happy for the first time. (*She takes the desk chair near to the low dining-table and sits*)

Mother He's begun to take an interest in life. Most unfortunate!

Selena enters and greets Mother

Selena Hello, everyone. Roger chickened out. Hello, Gran. What are we having today?

Mother *I'm* having yoghourt.

Selena Some people have all the luck. Hello, Mother.

Barnstable enters with a bottle of champagne and four bibs

Barnstable (*giving the bottle to Henry*) Sit down, Selena. How nice! You're wearing a hat! Your hair looks so much prettier when it's covered up. (*Selena is furious*) I'll get you a cushion, Henry. (*He goes to the bookcase*)

Henry I'm quite comfortable, thanks.

Barnstable fetches a cushion from the floor by the bookcase and hands it to Henry, who puts it behind his back

Barnstable No, no, Henry. (*He puts it on the floor, indicating that Henry should sit on it*)

Henry, looking dubious, does so

There you are. (*Getting a second cushion for Nora*) Nora, wouldn't you be more comfortable on one of these, instead of that old-fashioned chair? (*He raises her, puts down the cushion for her, and replaces the chair at the desk*)
Nora If you say so, dear.
Barnstable (*going*) Don't forget your bibs, everyone.

Barnstable exits

Nora and Selena put on their bibs

(*off*) Henry, put your bib on.

Henry Do you suppose he has second sight?
Nora I don't know. He meditates. And do you know he doesn't get indigestion any more.

Barnstable enters with four bowls

Selena New dishes, Pa?
Barnstable I bought them specially for the bouillabaisse.
Selena They look like dogs' dinner plates.
Barnstable They are! Now, put your bib on, Henry; you're worse than Adam.
Henry (*putting on his bib*) Do I need one with guttering?
Barnstable Not if you're a clean boy. Now, don't chatter; just sit quiet and let your gastric juices prepare to do their work.

Barnstable exits

Henry opens the champagne and serves it

Selena I wonder if it would help if we said grace?
Henry From what we are about to receive, good Lord rescue us.
Mother That sounds more like a prayer, Henry.
Nora It is Sunday, Mother.
Selena Sunday seems to come round quicker than it used to.
Nora Last Sunday wasn't too bad. I rather enjoyed my vol-au-vent.
Selena Roger was up half the night. If only there was something we could take beforehand.
Henry Entero-Vioform.

Barnstable enters with a tureen of bouillabaisse and ladle

Barnstable The bouillabaisse *au façon du chef*! Mother, see what you're missing! *Le patron mange ici!* (*To Henry*) Smell the sea!
Henry It's a guess, and only a guess—Thames Estuary?

Nora Shall I serve it, dear?

Barnstable No, no, I will. (*Serving them all*) The great thing is to have a bit of everything. I hope you all like squid. I don't bother with lobster. Snob stuff. Besides, I don't care for all that plunging into boiling water. Squids are different—they inspire hostility.

Henry You don't mind plunging them into boiling water?

Barnstable You don't have to. They arrive dead.

Henry Ominous!

Selena You've left the heads on.

Barnstable Certainly I've left the heads on. It particularly says leave the heads on. Pass the plate back, Selena, you haven't any mullet.

Selena I've got plenty, really.

Barnstable I insist. You can't enjoy bouillabaisse without mullet. That's the backbone, as it were. Mullet and squid. Enjoying your squid, Henry?

Henry You've put something in this.

Barnstable Of course, I've spent three and a half hours putting something in it.

Henry I can't quite distinguish the taste.

Barnstable One of the herbs? Basil?

Henry No.

Barnstable Fennel?

Henry No.

Barnstable Senna?

Henry I hope not!

Barnstable Ah, it must be the groundsel.

Henry Groundsel . . . What does it mean when a mussel doesn't open?

Barnstable I suppose it must have had a late night. Don't be silly Henry. Did you think it was bad luck?

Henry I thought it might be if you tried to break into it.

Nora That's funny!

Barnstable What's funny, dear?

Nora A pencil.

Barnstable In the bouillabaisse? Quite impossible, the whole thing is most carefully strain . . . (*He stops, and feels for a pencil in his pockets*) What sort of pencil?

Nora It's rather hard to tell.

Barnstable Ball point?

Nora (*fishing it out of her bowl*) It could have been a ball point, originally.

Barnstable Blast, that's my cooking pencil. (*Taking it and wiping it*) It must have dropped from my pocket. I expect it will dry out.

Henry Is it still in one piece?

Barnstable Don't worry, it wasn't expensive.

Henry I'm not worrying about your financial loss—but if the refill is floating around I'd rather like to know.

Barnstable looks at Selena

Selena It's rather like Christmas pudding, isn't it? You know, lucky

charms and sixpences. What do you suppose this is? (*She holds up
something from her bowl*)

Nora It's string, dear.

Henry Rubber band.

Barnstable Really, Henry, why should it be a rubber band? (*He takes it.
Clearly it is a rubber band*) It happens to be a piece of squid. (*Pushing it
into her mouth*) Chew it up well, Selena.

Nora I don't think she'd better, dear.

Barnstable Why not? It's the tough bits of squid people go for.

Henry Which people?

Barnstable People who appreciate bouillabaisse.

Mother (*very firmly*) I should spit it out, Selena, if I were you.

Selena (*doing so*) Sorry, Pa. I'll keep it as a souvenir.

Barnstable It's too ridiculous! People have simply forgotten how to chew.
I must say this is the best bouillabaisse I've eaten.

Nora How many have you eaten?

Barnstable Just this one. Do you think I should open a bistro? Barney's
Bistro?

Nora What for?

Barnstable It seems a pity to let my cooking be forgotten.

Henry I shall never forget it!

Barnstable You're not the public. I should like to show them what
cooking is all about. I don't know why people think it's difficult—it's
foolproof so long as you carefully follow instructions, and have the
courage to improvise.

Henry Like ball point pens?

Barnstable Don't go on about it, Henry, or I'll put it back! No, when I
went to the fishmonger yesterday he was out of sprats. I had to settle for
squids, whiting, mackerel and salted cod, but I knew something was
still lacking. On my way home, I passed the pet shop.

Henry That's where you bought the doggy bowls.

Barnstable And the goldfish.

Selena (*still eating*) Which goldfish, Pa?

Barnstable The ones you're eating now. I bought two dozen. The fellow
in the pet shop was quite excited. He kept asking me if I was sure they
were going to a happy home. (*Pause*) You should have seen his face
when I told him to wrap them.

They are all frozen in horror

Henry Barney, this time you really have poisoned us.

Selena I never heard of anyone eating goldfish.

Barnstable Cats eat them. They're always putting their paws in and
scooping them out.

Henry But cats have nine lives. If you'll excuse me, Barney . . . (*He rises*)

Barnstable Where are you going?

Henry I'm going to wash my paws.

Henry exits to the hall

Nora moves to the telephone

Nora I think I'd better ring Dr Burrows.
Barnstable Why?
Nora To tell him what's happened. Ask his advice. What did you do with them?
Barnstable Do with them?
Nora The goldfish.
Barnstable I cooked them.
Nora We know that, dear, but how did they die? Dr Burrows will want the facts. Were they fresh, do you suppose?
Mother They were alive this morning—I saw them swimming around quite happily.
Selena Why didn't you say something?
Mother I just thought Barney wanted to keep them as pets.
Barnstable So did they. Why should goldfish be different from any other fish?
Selena Father, there's a world food shortage. All over the world people have goldfish in bowls, ponds, fish-tanks and ornamental lakes.
Barnstable Well?
Selena If they had been edible, someone would have eaten them by now.
Mother I don't think you can argue that, Selena. There are lots of canaries in the world and people don't eat canaries.
Selena Father would. Wouldn't you, Pa?
Barnstable Possibly, as a starter. Don't throw anything away, Selena, I'm planning a cold fish soufflé.

Selena hastily exits

Nora Cold fish or goldfish?
Barnstable Really, Nora. I don't know what you're all so worried about. I looked them up in the *Encyclopaedia Britannica* this morning.
Nora To find out how to cook them?
Barnstable Among other things.
Mother Did it tell you?
Barnstable No, but it told me lots of other things. They were a species of carp, originally domesticated by the Chinese. They were introduced into France by the Goncourt Brothers as a present to Madame de Pompadour, and they have a life expectancy of thirty years.
Mother Not if you see them first.
Nora Hello, Dr Burrows. Sorry to disturb you, but my husband would like a word with you.
Barnstable I don't want to talk to him——
Nora Come on, Barney! Yes, my husband would like to ask you something.

Barnstable reluctantly comes to the phone

Now, Barney, be sure to tell him.

Barnstable (*taking over the phone*) Hello, Burrows—long time no see. What are you up to? . . . Lunch—so are we. What's your good lady giving you today? . . . Mutton, that's nice. We're having goldfish. . . . Goldfish . . . No, not on their own—in a bouillabaisse. It's a sort of fish stew. That's why we're phoning you. My wife finds them a little over-rich, and she was wondering if there was anything you think we should do after eating goldfish. . . . See a psychiatrist.

He is convulsed with laughter

(*Aside*) That's the first joke he's made for forty years. Someone must've paid his bill. (*In the phone*) She's got this ridiculous idea that goldfish are poisonous. . . . (*A pause, while he listens*) Well, that's your opinion and you're entitled to it.

He rings off, pauses, and then picks up the phone and starts to dial again

Perhaps I'd better ring the pet shop. They said they'd be standing by in case we wanted any more ant-eggs.

Nora What did Burrows say?

Barnstable Completely out of his depth. Thinks we're all right as long as they're British goldfish. If they come from abroad, we should go round to the School of Tropical Medicine for a check-up. . . . Is that Baines pet shop? Barnstable here. I don't know if you remember me. I bought two dozen goldfish yesterday. . . . Large? No, I thought they were rather small, considering the—— Oh, I see. (*Looking down at himself*) I'm on the generous side, yes. . . . Yes, thank you, they were delicious—I mean —delicious to see them floating—swimming about so happily. We wondered where they came from. Were they British goldfish or immigrant goldfish? You don't make any distinction. (*Aside*) One of those bloody do-gooders. (*On the phone*) I'm sure that's the right attitude. We just want to know where they came from. . . . Thank you. (*Replacing the receiver, to Nora reassuringly*) British. (*Pause*) From Hong Kong.

CURTAIN

SCENE 2

The same. One week later

The room is almost back to its original state, except for the mural in the recess

Barnstable and Henry are sitting on the sofa. Henry is looking at some X-rays

Henry By Jove!
Barnstable Well?

Henry I suppose it's bound to spread a little.

Barnstable It hasn't spread. You're looking at the first batch. This is the second batch, taken at the hospital last week.

Henry You've got them the wrong way round.

Barnstable I haven't. That's the hospital stamp and date.

Henry What happened, then?

Barnstable Either I've recovered from Blum's Disease, which the chap said was impossible, or . . .

Henry Or?

Barnstable I never had Blum's Disease in the first place.

Henry Bloody disgraceful! We should sue. (*He puts the X-rays separately on the coffee table*)

Barnstable Sue whom?

Henry The bloody doctor.

Barnstable Why should I sue him?

Henry Not you! Us! The last months—what we've been through—wrongful diagnosis, damage to our nervous systems, anxiety, distress, expense——! My God, if we were in America, we could make a fortune. We might get a bob or two here. Indigestion? (*No answer*) When did you know?

Barnstable Why should I sue? I've enjoyed the last eight months.

Henry *You* may have done, old son. No-one else has. If it wasn't Blum's Disease, why did you collapse?

Barnstable A week ago, at the Hospital for Tropical Medicine. They were going to use the stomach pump, and I told them they couldn't because I had Blum's Disease. They were frightfully excited. They'd never had a case before. They took an X-ray, and then woke me up at two in the morning to tell me I was cured.

Henry What did you say?

Barnstable I asked for a sleeping pill.

Henry Why?

Barnstable I was so excited I didn't think I'd be able to go to sleep again. They wanted to ring up Nora. I wouldn't let them.

Henry She still doesn't know?

Barnstable You're the one I thought I'd tell.

Henry First.

Barnstable Not necessarily first. Perhaps ever.

Henry But if you go on living, surely people will notice? There's nothing to be ashamed of, just because you had a fool of a doctor.

Barnstable Everyone is expecting me to die. Perhaps I ought to go through with it.

Henry You're going through with it one day. I mean, you're not proposing to live for ever, are you?

Barnstable Of course not.

Henry What you are announcing is not a cancellation, merely a postponement.

Barnstable That's one way of looking at it.

Henry You can't be sure—one can never be sure—you might step under a bus this afternoon on your way to the Round Pond.

Barnstable You think I should step under a bus?

Henry I don't know what you're going on about.

Barnstable Don't you? I'm going on about your reaction, Henry. When I told you that I wasn't going to die, if you'd given one tiny skip for joy, but all you said was sue the doctor.

Henry I was very angry with the doctor, but for you I am delighted.

Barnstable Are you?

Henry Of course. And that's why you've got to tell the family, because they'll be delighted too.

Barnstable Are you sure?

Henry Of course I'm sure.

Roger enters from the hall with a briefcase, some papers and a pen

Roger Hello, Henry. Ah, Father, glad to have caught you. I just want you to sign a cheque for me.

Henry Roger, your father has some news for you. Wonderful news. Shall I tell him, Barney, or will you?

Barnstable You tell him.

Henry Roger, what would be the most wonderful thing that could happen.

Roger To whom?

Henry To all of us. Your father, you, Nora, Selena, the family—well?

Roger Is it something to do with the business?

Henry In a way. It affects us all profoundly.

Roger Has it just been announced?

Henry More or less, wouldn't you agree, Barney?

Barnstable More or less.

Roger, the penny dropping, gets up and enthusiastically embraces his father

Roger Oh, Father, that's wonderful news! I'm so happy!

Barnstable So am I.

Roger I never thought you'd get planning permission.

Barnstable Planning permission?

Roger To pull down the house and develop the garden.

Barnstable I'm not planning to pull down the house.

Roger You signed the application form last month. He didn't read it of course. He was too busy painting. It was just the same when he sold the business.

Henry I didn't know you'd sold the business.

Barnstable Nor did I.

Roger As good as. There are a few formalities left.

Henry I think you're jumping the gun a bit, old son. The big news of the day is that your father hasn't got Blum's Disease.

Roger Since when?

Barnstable Since I came back from the hospital.

Roger But that's wonderful news, Father, I'm so happy for you. Just sign here, please. I always said you should get another opinion, and at last

you've taken my advice. Ah, thank you, Father. It is definite this time?
You're not going to change your mind again?

Henry He didn't change his mind. It was the doctor.

Roger Just as long as we know. Keep us in the picture and we can all
make plans. Have you told Mother?

Barnstable Not yet.

Roger The sooner the better, Father. She and Gran were going on a world
cruise next spring. I expect they can get a refund. Not to worry.

Barnstable I'm not worrying. I'm delighted.

Roger We all are. But Father, if you are going to be around for a while,
I wonder if you could cool it a bit.

Barnstable Cool it?

Roger Your extravagance. All these things you keep buying. Canvas,
paint, roller skates. It all adds up you know. And Vincent. He must cost
you a fortune in blood. I know we're selling the business, but I shall be
staying on as a director, and I shall have to plough back some of the
purchase price.

Barnstable What are you talking about? I'm not selling.

Roger What do you mean, Father? You're not thinking of coming
back?

Barnstable I haven't been away.

Roger Yes, you have. You've been away for a year, nearly.

Henry But it's his business.

Roger No, it isn't. It's Threlfall's business and mine.

Barnstable Threlfall's business?

Roger They made me an offer and I accepted it on your behalf.

Barnstable I'm not selling out to those crooks!

Roger I'm afraid it's too late. It's a *fait accompli* old son.

Barnstable Don't call me "old son". You're fired! I always knew it was a
mistake taking you into my business. You haven't got what it takes and
you don't want to learn. You and your smart-arsed accountants! You'd
better go back to something you really understand—mixed bathing!

Selena enters from the garden, with dry clothes

You're just in time, my girl.

Selena In time for what?

Henry The celebrations.

Barnstable I've been reprieved. I'm not ill. I'm going back to work.
Business as usual.

Selena Hang about a bit. I'm not with you.

Roger He's had some more X-rays taken. It was all a silly mistake.

Selena (*hugging him*) Oh, Father! I'm so happy.

Barnstable And I've sacked your husband.

Selena Oh, Father, I'm delighted.

Barnstable I knew you'd be pleased. Back to the Baths!

Selena No. Now he can start up on his own.

Roger Would you want me to?

Selena Of course. If your father isn't going to die, he can look after himself. You can look after Adam and me.

Roger I thought you didn't like me being in business.

Selena I've talked it over with Adam and he's changed my mind. He says you need a steady income.

Barnstable Adam's talking at last?

Selena He's been talking for some time.

Barnstable I never noticed.

Selena He didn't have anything to say to you, did he? But I have. Roger's done more for your business in six months than you ever did since you began. I don't say he'll put you out of business in a couple of years, because he's too nice for that, but he could if he wanted to, so watch out! Come on, Roger.

Selena exits to the hall

Roger Good-bye, Father. You know, it's a funny thing. To think of all the time I wasted trying to be a poet, and then suddenly I became one. Business is the real poetry of life. I never realized it before. The rhythm, the rhythm of going to the office, coming home, buying and selling, and knowing what you're doing is influencing other men's lives. If I make a killing in young broccoli today, my customers eat young broccoli tomorrow. But if I don't, they have to be content with brussels sprouts. Good luck with the business, old man.

Roger exits

Henry The Longfellow of the cabbage patch.

Barnstable (*sitting on the coffee table*) Fancy Nora and Mother planning a world cruise without taking me.

Henry You don't know they weren't taking you. (*He sits by Barnstable*) You said you wanted to be buried at sea. I expect they were going to scatter you off Hawaii. (*He gets up quickly*)

Barnstable What's the matter now?

Henry That could be very dangerous, sitting on X-rays. They could be radioactive. That was the silliest thing you ever did.

Barnstable (*getting up*) Why? We didn't sit on them for long.

Henry I mean sacking Roger. Ever since I've known you, you've been on at him to go into the business. He goes into the business, makes a success of it, and you sack him.

Barnstable Do you mind allowing me to handle my own affairs, for once? I don't know what makes you think you're such an expert in public relations. You're certainly not an expert with *my* relations. You've been a dead flop from the word go.

Henry What word go?

Barnstable When I told you I was dying, you started to plan a party.

Henry Well, I don't know what you're complaining about. You *had* a party. We all had the party. We've been having the bloody party for as long as I can remember. Now that the party's over, Barney, you don't have to go back to quarrelling with Roger.

Barnstable He won't leave. I'll give him a rise.

Henry And try and establish a meaningful relationship with him. You never seem able to do that with anyone for very long.

Barnstable I do. I had a very good meaningful relationship about nine months ago. It lasted one day. I'm beginning to feel the need of another one. I took your advice and had a look at the notice-boards. You were quite wrong, as usual. The first one I tried was, "Double Bed, Fully Sprung Mattress. Apply after Six".

Henry That should have been all right.

Barnstable It wasn't. I nearly had to buy the bed. After that, I went for "Keen Young Russian Student (Female) Desires English Coach One Night a Week". That sounded just my speed. It was in Bramerton Gardens, just round the corner. I hurried along. There was this beautiful girl. She asked me in, offered me coffee, asked if a pound an hour was fair. I thought it was too good to be true. Of course, it was. She started talking in Russian. I couldn't understand a word, and had to leave.

Henry There must be a funster operating in your district. My advice to you is to go west, old man—Soho. Or you might buy a copy of the *New Statesman*. They have some rather kinky ads. from time to time.

Barnstable If I have to buy the *New Statesman*, I shall give up sex.

Henry That might be best. Fascinating though I find your sex life, I must be getting on. May I say how genuinely thrilled and pleased I am to think we shall have your smiling old face around a bit longer; and let's hope it will be smiling a bit more often than it used to. You don't happen to remember the number in Bramerton Gardens, do you?

Barnstable Thirty-nine. Flat Three. Why?

Henry *Osta rojna Tovarich, polcovnik. Osta rojna.*

Henry kisses Barnstable on both cheeks and exits. Nora enters from the double-doors with a pill bottle

Nora You haven't taken your pills.

Barnstable I'll take them later.

Nora Feeling all right, dear?

Barnstable Quite all right thank you.

Nora I'm a bit worried about you. Since you came back from the hospital you haven't been quite your old self. You would tell me if you were in pain, or anything, wouldn't you?

Barnstable Yes, yes I would.

Nora sits at the desk to do her bills

As a matter of fact, I have got something to tell you.

Nora Yes, dear.

Barnstable Could I have your attention for a moment? It's rather important.

Nora Go on, dear, I'm listening.

Barnstable I had some more X-rays taken at the hospital. I haven't got
Blum's Disease. I haven't got anything. I may live to be a hundred. Did
you understand what I just said? Were you listening.

Long pause

Nora Yes, dear.
Barnstable Well?
Nora It's a bit of a shock.
Barnstable What did you say?
Nora I said it was a bit of a shock.
Barnstable Are you pleased?
Nora Of course I'm pleased. I'm delighted. It's just a bit of a shock.
Barnstable Don't keep on saying that.
Nora How long have you known?
Barnstable Ever since I came back from hospital.
Nora I don't understand why you didn't tell me. Aren't you thrilled?
Barnstable *I'm* thrilled. You're the ones who aren't thrilled. I told Henry,
he said I should sue the doctor. I told Roger, he said cool it. I tell you
and you say, "It's a bit of a shock".
Nora Have you told Mother?
Barnstable Not yet.
Nora She'll be thrilled.
Barnstable I wouldn't bank on it.

Nora goes to the door and calls

Nora Mother! Mother!
Mother (*off*) I'm washing-up, dear. What is it?
Nora Come in here a moment. Barney's something to tell you. You must
break it to her gently, Barney. You know she's got a weak heart.
Barnstable I'd rather not break it to her at all. She'll only say she knew it
all the time.
Nora Of course you must tell her.

Mother comes in with a tea-towel

Now, sit down, Mother.
Mother I'll sit down when I've done the washing-up.
Nora No, sit down, dear.

Mother sits down

Barnstable I'd better give her some brandy. We don't want her ticker
playing her up again as it did at the whist drive. A handful of trumps
and they all went on the floor.

Barnstable is pouring a glass of brandy which he brings to Mother

We've got some news for you, Mother.

Mother takes a sip of the brandy

At the hospital, they took some more X-rays——

Mother I know, dear. And you're cured.

Furious, Barnstable takes the glass away from her and pours the brandy back into the bottle

Dr Burrows told me. I didn't mention it. I thought you wanted to keep it a secret.

Nora (*quite angry*) Mother, I really do think you might have told me!

Barnstable Yes, you should have done, Mother. It might have saved her a shock.

Nora That's not fair, Barney. You'd no right to spring it on me like that.

Barnstable Spring it on you? I've waited a whole bloody week! I don't say I expected a party and general rejoicing, but I did expect someone to be pleased—even to congratulate me.

Mother Don't shout, dear. We can hear you perfectly well.

Barnstable I'm shouting for joy, Mother, because I've been reprieved. I'm sorry to disappoint you all, but I'm going on living. You'll just have to get used to it.

Nora bursts into tears and runs out to the hall. Mother stands up

Mother Now you've upset Nora.

Barnstable *I've* upset *her*? *She's* upset *me*!

Mother You've upset yourself, dear. You always do. You'd better go and apologize.

Barnstable I shan't do anything of the kind. For heaven's sake, sit down, Mother, and let's discuss this wonderful news.

Mother No, thank you, dear. I've better things to do.

Barnstable What?

Mother I haven't finished the washing-up.

Barnstable You're the most heartless woman I've ever met. You're supposed to be my mother.

Mother I *am* your mother. Don't speak to your mother like that, even in fun. And if you won't apologize to Nora, you might at least tidy up this room. You know how it upsets her, the way you leave all this rubbish lying about. (*She starts to go*)

Barnstable They happen to be my X-rays.

Mother Well, we don't want them in the drawing-room, dear.

Mother exits

Barnstable You don't want *me* in the drawing-room, either.

Barnstable picks up the X-rays and tries unsuccessfully to tear them. He goes to the desk, brings out the wastepaper-basket from under it, stuffs the X-rays in, takes out a box of matches, and is about to strike one

Poppy enters from the garden. She is carrying a baby in a carry-cot, and a plastic bag with a bottle, baby-powder and other necessities

Poppy Having a bonfire? Nice!

Barnstable Poppy!! What are you doing? How lovely to see you. Is that your baby?

Poppy Three weeks old today. (*She puts the bag down where Barnstable does not see it*)

Barnstable (*suddenly wary*) Is it, now? (*Counting on his fingers*) That's nice. A little girl?

Poppy Boy. Remind you of anyone? (*She puts the baby on the coffee table*)

Barnstable No, of course not. I mean, they're all supposed to look like Winston Churchill. What's his name? He's splendid.

Poppy I haven't given him one, yet. Any suggestions?

Barnstable Me? No, I wouldn't presume. That's something you'll have to decide for yourself. For yourselves.

Poppy How are we, then?

Barnstable Me? Oh! I'm holding my own pretty well. I might go off at any moment, and then again, I might not. It's something I've learnt to live with. More of a strain for my family. I've put my affairs in order; there's not much more I can do. More important, tell me about yourself. What have you been up to?

Poppy You can see what I've been up to.

Barnstable Yes, of course. Are we married?

Poppy No.

Barnstable Nobody seems to want to get married any more. It's something we old fuddy-duddies have got to get used to.

Poppy I'd like to get married.

Barnstable But he doesn't want to?

Poppy Who doesn't want to?

Barnstable The father of your child.

Poppy I haven't asked him. He's married already.

Barnstable Is he, now? Has he got a family?

Poppy (*gazing fondly at her child*) Just one son. (*She looks at Barnstable*) Are you all right?

Barnstable Me? Yes, it's just a bit of a shock seeing you again—seeing both of you.

Poppy I'm sorry.

Barnstable Please don't apologize—the boot is entirely on the other leg. I mean, if there's anything I can do to help, you can count on me.

Poppy Can I? Can I, really?

Barnstable Up to a point, that is. Of course, I'll do what I can, naturally. Placed as I am, I have to be a bit careful. My son's running the business and he just lets me have pocket money. Have you somewhere to stay.

Poppy We have a house—a commune. (*She sits on the sofa*) We're squatting.

Barnstable Isn't it rather difficult to squat with a three-week-old baby?

Poppy No, he doesn't want much—just a meal now and then. I really ought to give him a bit now. Would you mind?

Barnstable No, of course not. I must say, you young people really are marvellous—the way you take it all in your stride. (*Seeing her undoing her blouse*) Not here!

Poppy No?

Barnstable Mother, again, I'm afraid. She's very old fashioned.

Poppy This has been going on for quite a time, you know.

Barnstable I think she's forgotten the system. Besides, she thinks you're a young man who works in a garage. She'd be a bit surprised to find you topping up a baby.

Poppy I can give him a bottle, if you like.

Barnstable That would be better.

Poppy Hold on, it's in the pram. I won't be a jiffy.

Barnstable Shall I bring little. . . ?

Poppy has gone out to the garden

Barnstable inspects the baby. He goes to the wall mirror and looks at himself, lifts the mirror down, carries it to the coffee table. He puts it by the baby and looks at it, comparing his own reflection with the baby

Nora enters, sees him, and watches for a second

Nora What are you doing?

Barnstable (*taken unawares*) Baby-sitting.

Nora Whose baby is it?

Barnstable I'm not sure. At least I know the mother. She's a Miss Seed.

Nora Who's the father?

Barnstable I didn't ask. She's gone to get a bottle.

Nora Where from?

Barnstable The pram, it's outside.

Nora Does she work in your office?

Barnstable Good heavens! Why should you think that? No, of course not, she's just a friend. I met her—somewhere or other.

Nora Now she's gone for a bottle?

Barnstable That's right.

Nora Which is in the pram outside? (*Producing a bottle from the bag Barnstable never noticed*) Like this, for instance?

Barnstable Where did you find that?

Nora With these. (*She unpacks more baby kit, such as nappies, talcum powder, etc*)

Barnstable I'd better go and tell her. These young people are so scatter-brained. Poppy! (*Realizing*) Miss Seed!

Barnstable exits to the garden

Nora examines the baby

Barnstable returns

That's funny. She isn't there.

Nora Did you find the pram, dear?

Barnstable No pram, either.

Nora Fancy.

Barnstable What could have happened to her?

Nora How well do you know her?

Barnstable Just to say "Hullo" to. A bit better than that perhaps.

Nora It's not your baby, is it, dear?

Barnstable Of course not. What on earth makes you think such a thing?

Nora If you're going to abandon your baby, I suppose the father is not a bad person to abandon it on.

Barnstable What makes you think she's abandoned it, dear?

Nora I heard the car drive off.

Barnstable What do you think we ought to do?

Nora You could take him round to the police station.

Barnstable There's no reason to have him arrested.

Nora Perhaps they'll find the father.

Barnstable Ah, well, I suppose there's just a million-to-one chance it could be me.

Nora A million-to-one hardly counts.

Barnstable A bit less, possibly, one in ten thousand. I did go to bed with her.

Nora You and ten thousand others?

Barnstable Once. On the spur of the moment, when I thought I was dying. She was going to witness my will, then we changed our plans. I'm not making excuses. I don't regret it. But if he goes out of this house I shall go with him, just in case he is mine.

Nora Where to?

Barnstable To a nursing home. I wouldn't mind a rest. Nor would he, I daresay, poor little so-and-so. He's squatting somewhere or other, at the moment. Perhaps Roger and Selena would like to have a brother for Adam. By Jove, that's a solution. I mean, nowadays, parents are always getting landed with their unmarried kids' children. This is the same thing in reverse.

Nora How does it feel to know you're a father after thirty years?

Barnstable I don't *know*. It's only a guess. Do you think he looks like me?

Nora Not at all.

Barnstable There you are. I'm pretty sure he's not mine.

Nora What's he doing here, then?

Barnstable Any port in a storm, I suppose. Look here, let's not concern ourselves with whose baby he is; or rather, let's assume he is mine. That way, we can look after him without bothering with adoption societies and so on. Start again. You were never happier than when Roger was a baby. A baby in the home is better than the television. Good for Mother, it might slow her down. Good for you, good for all of us. What do you say?

Nora No. This time, Barney, you've gone too far. I'm not prepared to start again, as you put it, with someone else's baby.

Barnstable It's not exactly someone else's.

Nora I'm not at all sure I'm prepared to start again with you. For more than a week, now, you've let me think you were dying when you were perfectly well, and now you calmly announce you're a father and expect me to become a mother.

Barnstable It was only a suggestion. I thought it might amuse you.

Nora Well, it doesn't amuse me one little bit.

Barnstable Well, what would you like me to do? I just want to fit in with everyone's plans. It's no good adopting a negative attitude in these matters. Here we are with a baby, apparently. What are we going to do?

Nora Don't you mean, what are *you* going to do?

Barnstable looks at her horrified

Poppy enters with a tin of baby food

Barnstable Poppy! Oh, well done! We were just beginning to wonder what had happened to you, weren't we, dear?

Poppy I had to find a chemist.

Barnstable This is my wife, Nora. Nora—Poppy.

Poppy Hi!

Nora Hi!

Poppy Has he been behaving himself?

Nora Has who—— Oh, the baby. Yes, indeed. He's asleep. Would you like to boil a kettle?

Poppy If he's asleep I'll feed him later in the car. We don't want to miss the ferry. We're off to Cuba.

Barnstable (*relieved*) Cuba? Are you? I mean, I remember your saying you wanted to go to Cuba, last time we met.

Poppy Did you ever get to Bognor Regis?

Barnstable No. We got to a lot of other places, didn't we, dear?

Nora Oh, yes. Stoke Poges, Golder's Green Crematorium, Brookwood.

Barnstable Yes, well, it doesn't matter. I wish I was going to Cuba with you.

Poppy So do I.

Nora (*suddenly*) Why don't you go with her?

Barnstable It's not possible, alas. I can't suddenly go off to Cuba—just like that.

Nora Why not?

Barnstable Well, I haven't got a passport, have I?

Nora Yes, you have.

Barnstable I'll need a visa.

Nora You could get one.

Barnstable But do you want me to go to Cuba?

Nora Yes, I do, Barney. I want you to go very much.

Barnstable Why?

Nora You told me just now you wanted to fit in with everyone's plans. My plan for you is *Cuba*.

Barnstable (*hedging*) I don't know that Miss Seed wants me to go with her.

Nora She just said she did, didn't you?

Poppy I'd love you to come, if you want to.

Barnstable What about Mother, poor old lady?

Nora You want to take her, too?

Barnstable Of course I don't. I'm wondering how she'd feel about this. Badly, I'm afraid.

Nora At first, perhaps, but I'm sure she'll manage without you, for a bit. I'm sure we all shall.

Barnstable Anyone would think, dear, you want to get rid of me.

Nora I do. I do want to get rid of you for a time.

Barnstable All right. A nod's as good as a wink, as far as I'm concerned. If that's your little game. I'll play it for you. You think I'm bluffing now. I'm not, you know. I've been living in a bit of a fool's paradise, believing I was wanted at last. This afternoon, I got the message.

Poppy You are wanted.

Barnstable Yes, I believe I am. I think I'd like to come straight away. I'll put a few things together and we'll be off. (*To Nora*) Perhaps you'd like to tell Mother. I'm sure you're right—she'll manage without me. I'm sure you all will. (*He goes to the door*)

Nora Barney!

Barnstable Yes?

Barnstable quickly turns back

Nora Shall I help you pack?

Barnstable (*furious*) No, thank you. I'll manage.

Barnstable exits to the hall

Nora What made you decide to pay us a visit?

Poppy George and I just happened to be passing, and I saw the name of the road. I thought Barney would like to see the baby—cheer him up.

Nora Who's George?

Poppy He's my fellow. I don't know how he's going to feel about Barney coming along, but I'll explain how things are. I expect he'll understand. There's just one thing, what am I to do with the ashes?

Nora The ashes? He's not expecting to win those is he?

Poppy Barney's ashes. You want him to die in the sun, isn't that it? Isn't that why you want him to come to Cuba? Enjoy his life up to the last.

Nora He isn't dying any longer. Didn't he tell you he's cured?

Poppy You mean we've got him for keeps? I don't think George will like that much. I'd have to ask him.

Nora You do that while my husband is packing.

Poppy George is like me—he travels light.

Poppy exits to the garden

Nora sits at the desk and starts doing her accounts

Mother enters through the double doors on her way to the garden. She carries a trug and secateurs. She double-takes on seeing the baby

Mother There's a baby on the table.
Nora It's Barney's, Mother. He's taking it to Cuba. At least, he was taking it to Cuba—now there's a hitch. George has to be consulted.
Mother Who's George? You don't have to tell me, dear, if you don't want to.
Nora I don't mind telling you, but it's rather complicated. I thought I'd pay a few bills, while I was waiting.
Mother Waiting for what?
Nora Everyone to make up their minds.

Barnstable enters, dressed in a hectic Miami-beach set, with tin helmet and haversack

Barnstable Cuba, here I come!
Nora (*casually glancing up*) Very nice, dear.
Barnstable What are you doing, Mother?
Mother Admiring my new grandson—he's very like you.
Barnstable (*furiously*) Did you have to tell her, Nora?
Nora She asked.
Mother What's all this about your emigrating to Cuba? Bit late in the day, isn't it?
Barnstable I'm not emigrating, I'm going there on a visit, at Nora's request.
Mother Oh, you're both going?
Barnstable No, Mother. I am going with the mother of my child. I have, as it were, temporarily, and by popular request, swapped families.
Nora I wouldn't count on it.
Mother Apparently, it all depends on George.
Barnstable Who's George?

George enters, followed by Poppy. He now has long hair and trendy clothes

Poppy George says Cuba is O.K. He says Castro needs all the volunteers he can get.
Barnstable I'm not planning to volunteer for Castro.
George You don't have to volunteer, man. You are a volunteer. All the workers in Cuba are volunteers. It's the system, man.
Mother Barney. Introduce us.
Barnstable My mother. My wife. I haven't the slightest idea who he is.
George Stubbs. Two-eight-six M.P. That's the name you knew me under.
Barnstable That's right. He was a policeman.
Mother Oh, I see. You're a detective in plain clothes, well, nearly plain. I've read about it.

Poppy No, he's resigned. We met on a demo. 'Course, we were on different sides, then.

Barnstable You slapped his face again?

Poppy No, another pig slapped mine, and he didn't like that, so he hit the other pig, and that's how it all started.

Mother Quite a farmyard romance!

Nora If you've resigned, should you be wearing that jacket?

George If the fuzz want to make something of it, they can.

Nora Did it take you long to learn to speak like that?

George No time at all. It's easy, much easier than trying to keep your temper and hold back the crowds and not return the stones when they're thrown at you. I mean, that's not my idea of a good time. But fuzz-baiting, that's something else—that is fun. Bashing the pigs, putting the boot in. You take to it like a duck to water.

Mother I'm sure you do. (*To Poppy*) You're a very lucky young man!

Poppy Come on, George, Cuba's waiting!

Mother You're not really taking my grandson? I don't think that's very wise. Barney, yes—he's quite old enough to look after himself; but not this little comrade.

George Your grandson, madam? Oh, I see. (*To Poppy, indicating Barnstable*) You gave *him* the benefit of the doubt this time.

Poppy I didn't give it him—he took it.

George I shouldn't count on it, if I were you. Anyway, he's mine now. He's on my passport. It's official.

Poppy What does it matter who the father is? The important thing is that we all love him. (*To Mother*) Good-bye. This is for you. (*She hands her a flower. To Nora*) Good-bye, Mrs Barney. I think you're doing the right thing. Make a clean break. When it's over, it's over. Come on, George, bring—Liberation.

Poppy exits to the garden

George Liberation. Liberation Stubbs. Like it! Like it! (*He hands the baby to Barnstable, then puts his arm round Barnstable's shoulder and moves with him towards the garden. To Mother*) Cheers, darling! (*To Nora*) See you, sweetheart!

George and Barnstable exit to the garden. Barnstable holding the carry-cot with one hand and giving the clenched fist salute with the other

Nora You don't think he'll really go?

Mother (*going to the drinks cabinet*) That was your idea, wasn't it, dear?

Nora I was trying to give him back some sense of responsibility. I didn't expect him to go through with it.

Mother I don't suppose they'll take him, for a moment.

Nora Do you think he's quite right in the head?

Mother I never thought him quite right in the head.

Nora Those two seem as mad as he is. What on earth could he do in Cuba?

Mother Work in the sugar canes. Prepare for the world revolution. Perhaps they'll infiltrate him back here and we shall have to go to Bow Street and bail him out.

A car is heard driving away

Nora That was the car. (*Pause*) He's gone. He's really gone. And he never even said good-bye.

Barnstable enters from the garden

Mother nudges Nora. Barnstable crosses the room in silence and sits in the armchair

Mother (*after a pause*) Changed your mind, dear?

Barnstable I didn't think I'd be very comfortable in the boot!

Nora Wouldn't you feel more comfortable, now, without the haversack?

Barnstable gets up and takes the haversack off

Mother You wouldn't have enjoyed it as much as you think. Carmen Miranda is dead.

Nora And they've closed the casinos.

Mother Barney's given up gambling, haven't you, dear?

Barnstable Who says I've given it up? Who says I've given anything up? You know what I'm going to do? I'm going to launch my new racing-yacht.

Nora In that hat?

Barnstable Certainly in this hat. The way things are at the Round Pond it'll come in handy.

Mother Be careful crossing the High Street; we don't want you knocked down by a bus.

Barnstable Why does everyone think I'll get knocked down by a bus?

Mother Because you will dart across the road and not wait for the lights.

Barnstable (*picking up the model yacht from the cabinet*) I don't cross by the lights.

Mother You should. Wait for the little green man. You always used to.

Barnstable I had more time in those days.

Mother You've got more time now.

Barnstable I've got out of the habit.

Mother Don't be so selfish. I always think it's such bad luck on the drivers when they run over people.

Barnstable That's one way of looking at it. Can I go now, please?

Mother Run along and enjoy yourself, and don't forget, look left, look right, look left again.

Barnstable I'll remember, Mother.

Barnstable exits to the hall

Nora Mother, dear, it's look right, look left, look right again.

Mother Why didn't you say so, dear?

Nora I thought there'd been enough argument for one afternoon.

Mother Too late now. Look right, look left, look—— You're right, of course. Oh well, not to worry. If anything should happen, it would be the first time he'd listened to my advice.

There is the sound of screeching brakes and a loud car crash. Mother and Nora jump up

Nora Barney!

Mother You don't think. . . ?

Nora I'll go.

Mother We'll go together.

Mother and Nora turn to the door

Barnstable enters with the yacht broken in two pieces

Barnstable Mother, in a one-way street, it's look right, look right, look right again!

CURTAIN

FURNITURE AND PROPERTY LIST

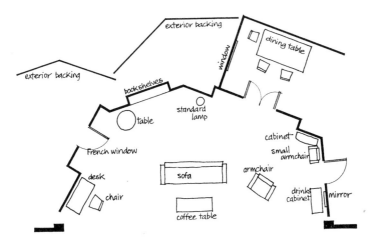

ACT I

SCENE 1

On stage: Desk. *On it:* telephone, writing materials, bills. *Under it:* wastepaper
basket. *On floor beside it:* box of toys

Circular table (in window). *On it:* photo of Barnstable, pile of newspapers, bowl of artificial flowers

Bookshelves. *In them:* books, including set of *Encyclopaedia Britannica*

Cabinet. *On it:* bowl of artificial flowers

Drinks cabinet. *On it:* tray, whisky, sherry, gin, glasses. *On floor
beside it:* toys, including Klondike Willy. *Over it:* wall mirror

Coffee table. *On it:* 2 X-ray plates, for **Henry**, brandy bottle, 2 brandy
balloons

Desk chair

Sofa. *On it:* cushions

Armchair

Small armchair

Carpet

Window curtains

DINING-ROOM ANNEX
Dining-table
3 small chairs

Off stage: Bundle of cleaned clothing **(Selena)**
              Clothes from washing **(Nora)**
              Pair of tweezers **(Roger)**
              Bottle of lotion, cotton-wool **(Nora)**

Personal: **Henry:** notebook, pencil
              Barnstable: wallet with £10 note, watch

SCENE 2

Strike: Toy box
              Brandy and glasses
              Newspapers
              Clothing
              Change artificial flowers

Set: Desk tidy
              Box of chocolates on coffee table
              Will on chair for **Henry**

Off stage: Briefcase, umbrella **(Roger)**
              Mother's spectacles **(Barnstable)**

Personal: **Henry:** wallet with £10 note
              Barnstable: watch

ACT II

SCENE 1

Strike: Armchair
              Coffee table
              Books and shelves
              Pictures
              Window table
              Change artificial flowers

Set: Jazzy cover on sofa
              Small chair by drinks table
              Bat in cage with cloth over
              Model yacht on cabinet
              2 large cushions on floor by bookshelf alcove
              Wine rack in place of bookshelves
              Buddha on cabinet
              Erotic mural in dining-room
              Palette and painting materials on dining-room table
              Easel and painting in dining-room
              Ultra-modern abstracts on walls and against sofa and furniture—also
                  one nude
              Bow and arrow in dining-room
              Roller-skate by sofa

Off stage: Low circular dining-table with jazzily painted top **(Henry, Barnstable)**
4 mats, 4 spoons, 4 forks, 4 glasses **(Barnstable)**
Tray and 4 glasses **(Nora)**
Bottle of wine in cradle **(Barnstable)**
Container of blood **(Barnstable)**
Dish of yoghourt and spoon **(Mother)**
Bottle of champagne **(Barnstable)**
4 bibs **(Barnstable)**
4 bowls, pencil concealed in one, rubber-band in another **(Barnstable)**
Tureen and ladle **(Barnstable)**

SCENE 2

Strike: Low dining-table with all dishes, etc.
Large cushions
Buddha
Painting materials
Easel
Loose paintings
Bow and arrow
Roller-skate
Change artificial flowers

Set: Armchair in former position, with new, quiet cover
Matching cover on sofa
Room generally tidier
Original coffee table
Replace small armchair in former position
2 X-rays on sofa for **Henry**
Bills on desk

Off stage: Briefcase, pen, cheque **(Roger)**
Clean washing **(Selena)**
Pill bottle **(Nora)**
Tea towel **(Mother)**
Baby in carry-cot **(Poppy)**
Plastic bag with baby bottle, talcum powder, etc. **(Poppy)**
Tin of baby food **(Poppy)**
Trug and secateurs **(Mother)**
Tin helmet **(Barnstable)**
Haversack **(Barnstable)**
Model yacht broken in two pieces **(Barnstable)**

Personal: **Barnstable:** box of matches

LIGHTING PLOT

Property fittings required: 2 table lamps, 1 standard lamp (dressing only)
Interior. A living-room. The same scene throughout

ACT I, SCENE 1

To open: General effect of warm autumn sunshine
No cues

ACT I, SCENE 2

To open: As Scene 1
No cues

ACT II, SCENE 1

To open: General effect of bright spring sunshine
No cues

ACT II, SCENE 2

To open: As Act II, Scene 1
No cues

EFFECTS PLOT

ACT I

Scene 1

No cues

Scene 2

No cues

ACT II

Scene 1

No cues

Scene 2

Cue 1   **Mother:** "... and bail him out."   (Page 59)
           Sound of car starting up and driving away

Cue 2   **Mother:** "... listened to my advice."   (Page 60)
           Sound of screeching brakes and loud car crash

MADE AND PRINTED IN GREAT BRITAIN BY
LATIMER TREND & COMPANY LTD PLYMOUTH

MADE IN ENGLAND